AMERICAN
Headway

Proven success beyond the classroom

THIRD EDITION

Workbook

Liz and John Soars

OXFORD
UNIVERSITY PRESS

Contents

Go to **iChecker** Online Self-Assessment to access the **audio**, **Progress Checks**, and **Spotlight on Testing** for test preparation lessons.

1

A world of difference

Tenses – auxiliary verbs • Prepositions • Introduction
• Phonetic Symbols • Vowel sounds

🎧 When you see this symbol, go to iChecker to listen to the audio.

Tenses

1 Recognizing tenses

Read the text. Use the verb forms in *italics* to complete the chart.

Simple Present (x 4)
works

Present Continuous (x 1)

Simple Past (x 3)

Past Continuous (x 1)

Present Perfect (x 1)

Present Perfect Continuous (x 1)

Future forms (x 2)

Simple Present passive (x 1)

Simple Past passive (x 1)

CHICAGO – MY KIND OF TOWN

Chicago is the third largest global city in the United States. Why do so many immigrants come to the Windy City?

WEI ZHANG, 32, from China, *works* in the city. He says, "I *love* living in Chicago. It's dynamic and extremely international. People *come* here to find work but then realize that it's really exciting. My company *is owned* by a Chinese bank, and I'*m going out* with an American woman. I'*ll stay* here for another five or six years."

SOFIA SANTOYO, 21, from Brazil, *came* to Chicago three years ago to learn English and *has been* here ever since. "I *met* my boyfriend while I *was working* at the Drake Hotel. I *was employed* in Accounts. I now think of Chicago as my home. We'*re going to get* married next year."

FRANCESCO ROSSI, 28, from Italy, *found* a job in two weeks. "Unemployment is high in Italy, especially for young people. I *know* friends in Rome who *have been looking* for work for months," she said. "There is a sense of opportunity here in Chicago. Anything is possible."

2 Producing tenses

Complete the sentences using the verb in the box and the tense given.

make

1 SIMPLE PRESENT

   I work for a company that _____makes_____ printers.

2 SIMPLE PRESENT PASSIVE

   The printers _____ in China.

3 PRESENT PERFECT

   We _____ a big profit this year.

take

4 SIMPLE PAST

   I _____ my daughter to the zoo yesterday.

5 *GOING TO* FUTURE

   I _____ her to the movies tonight.

6 SIMPLE PAST PASSIVE

   This photo of her _____ on vacation last year.

be

7 PRESENT PERFECT

   I _____ to every country in Asia on business.

8 SIMPLE PAST

   This time last year I _____ in Thailand.

9 *WILL* FUTURE

   Next week I _____ in Mexico.

work

10 PRESENT CONTINUOUS

   I _____ at home this week.

11 PAST CONTINUOUS

   I _____ in Boston the week before last.

12 PRESENT PERFECT CONTINUOUS

   I'm tired. I _____ hard recently.

3 Tenses and time expressions

Put the verb in the correct tense for the time expressions.

1 He usually _goes_ (go) jogging ...

   > every day.
   > twice a week.
   > on Friday mornings.

2 I _____ (go) to Florida ...

   > last year.
   > in 2014.
   > six months ago.

3 We _____ (live) here ...

   > for five years.
   > since July.
   > all our lives.

4 What _____ you _____ (do) ...

   > right now?
   > these days?
   > this week?

5 I _____ (see) you ...

   > next week.
   > later.
   > tonight.

Auxiliary verbs

4 Auxiliary verb or full verb?

Is the verb in **bold** used as an **auxiliary** verb (**A**) or a **full** verb (**F**)?

1 [A] **Have** you ever been to China?
   [F] They **have** three children.

2 [ ] I **do** my homework every night.
   [ ] Where **do** you come from?

3 [ ] They **are** nice children.
   [ ] They **are** learning English.

4 [ ] What time **did** you get home?
   [ ] We **did** a play at school today.

5 [ ] Brazil **has** won the World Cup five times.
   [ ] Brazil **has** some beautiful beaches.

6 [ ] I **was** having dinner at 8:00.
   [ ] I **was** at home.

7 [ ] My sister **does** yoga every week.
   [ ] What **does** your father do?

8 [ ] My son **is** at school.
   [ ] He **is** taught Spanish by my old teacher.

5 Asking questions

1 Read the *Amazing facts*. Some information is missing. Write questions to get the information.

Amazing facts

1 The human heart beats _____ times a year.

2 The solar system was formed _____ years ago.

3 _____ people are born every day.

4 Oil was first discovered in Saudi Arabia in _____ .

5 The U.S. spends _____ on defense every year.

6 Right now, the International Space Station is flying at _____ .

7 Shakespeare had _____ children.

8 _____ people were killed in the Second World War.

9 The U.S. President earns _____ a year.

10 The average marriage in the U.S. lasts _____ years.

1 How many **times does the human heart beat a year** ?

2 How long ago _____ ?

3 How many _____ ?

4 When _____ ?

5 How much _____ ?

6 How fast _____ ?

7 How many _____ ?

8 How many _____ ?

9 How much _____ ?

10 How long _____ ?

2 🎧 Listen, check, and complete the text with the answers you hear.

6 Replying with questions

Reply to these statements with a question.

1 Joan's writing an e-mail.
   Who's **she writing to** ?

2 David speaks four languages.
   Which _____ ?

3 I got some great presents for my birthday.
   What _____ ?

4 Joy and Eric paid a lot of money for their house.
   How much _____ ?

5 I'm going to the movies tonight.
   What _____ ?

6 We had a wonderful vacation.
   Where _____ ?

7 Bye! See you later!
   Where _____ ?

8 Jamal's talking on the phone.
   Who _____ ?

7 Negatives

Everything that **A** says is wrong! Complete **B**'s lines as she corrects him.

1 **A** Jane and Ann live in the center of town.
   B **They don't live in the center** . They live in the suburbs!

2 **A** They had a great vacation.
   B _____ . It rained every day!

3 **A** Jane works in an office.
   B _____ . She's a teacher!

4 **A** Ann has a brother.
   B _____ . She's an only child!

5 **A** They've shared an apartment for years.
   B _____ . They only met last August!

6 **A** They have a lot of friends.
   B _____ . They don't know anybody!

7 **A** Jane went to college.
   B _____ . She left school at 16!

8 **A** Ann has to work at night.
   B _____ . She's a librarian!

8 Short answers

Read the conversation. Complete the sentences with short answers.

S Hi, Amy. I haven't seen you for ages. Have you been away?

A (1) Yes, *I have* . I've been in Australia for six months.

S Wow! Did you have a good time?

A (2) Yes, _____ . It was amazing.

S Were you traveling around?

A (3) No, _____ . When I first got there, I stayed in Sydney for three months.

S Don't your aunt and uncle live there?

A (4) Yes, _____ . I stayed with them for a few weeks, then I got a place of my own with friends.

S Did you rent an apartment?

A (5) No, we _____ . We rented a house near the beach. Then we went up the east coast.

S And what did you think of Australians? They're really nice, aren't they?

A (6) Yes, _____ . Very easy going.

S Don't they spend a lot of time outdoors in the sunshine?

A (7) Yes, _____ . But the sun doesn't shine all the time. On the way back I went to Thailand. Have you been there?

S (8) No, _____ . But I'd love to. What are you doing now? Are you looking for a job?

A (9) Yes, _____ . But it isn't easy. Do you have any ideas where I could look?

S (10) No, _____ . Sorry. But I'm sure you'll manage. Anyway, Amy, it's good to see you again.

A Thanks. And you. I'll see you around. Bye!

🎧 Listen and check.

Pronunciation

9 Phonetic symbols – vowel sounds

1 Look at the symbols for vowel sounds.

Short vowel sounds					
/ɪ/	/ɛ/	/æ/	/ɔ/	/ʊ/	/ʌ/
big	pen	cat	dog	put	sun
_____	_____	_____	_____	_____	_____
_____	_____	_____	_____	_____	_____

Long vowel sounds				
/i/	/ɑr/	/ɔr/	/u/	/ər/
see	car	more	two	bird
_____	_____	_____	_____	_____
_____	_____	_____	_____	_____

🎧 Listen and repeat.

2 Write these words under the correct symbol in the chart in exercise 1.

push	heart	red	cool	saw	eat
ran	war	hit	first	bus	build
friend	group	foot	black	wash	does
meet	start	short	work		

🎧 Listen, check, and repeat.

▶▶ **Phonetic Symbols p. 93**

10 Word stress

🎧 Listen and put the words in the correct column according to the stress pattern.

typical	education	foreign	immediate
ambitious	regret	Internet	economic
sunshine	reception	correct	community

1 ●●   country   _____ _____

2 •●   polite   _____ _____

3 •●•   important   _____ _____

4 ●••   grandfather   _____ _____

5 ••●•   population   _____ _____

6 •●••   experience   _____ _____

Vocabulary

11 Grammar words

Match words in **A** with a grammar term in **B**.

A		B	
1	**f** write, want	a	preposition (prep)
2	she, him	b	adjective (adj)
3	car, tree	c	adverb (adv)
4	can, must	d	modal auxiliary verb
5	slowly, always	e	pronoun (pron)
6	nice, pretty	f	full verb
7	bigger, older	g	count noun (C)
8	to like	h	noncount noun (U)
9	a	i	comparative adjective
10	on, at, under	j	superlative adjective
11	hoping, living	k	infinitive with *to* (infin with *to*)
12	the	l	*-ing* form of the verb (*-ing* form)
13	fastest, hottest	m	past participle (pp)
14	done, broken	n	definite article
15	rice, weather	o	indefinite article

12 Word formation

Complete the sentences using the word in CAPITALS in the correct form.

1 My brother is a **musician** . MUSIC

2 A trumpet is a _____ instrument. MUSIC

3 I drive a very _____ car. ECONOMY

4 I spend more than I earn. I must _____ . ECONOMY

5 _____ give governments advice about finance. ECONOMY

6 _____ have a lot of responsibility for their staff. EMPLOY

7 The _____ rate in the U.S. is about 5%. EMPLOY

8 I'm self-_____ . I don't work for anyone else. EMPLOY

13 Words that go together

Match a word in **A** with a line in **B**.

A		B	
1	**b** go	a	a business
2	make	b	online
3	win	c	a photograph
4	start	d	home
5	take	e	archaeology
6	do	f	a prize
7	study	g	an appointment
8	leave	h	your best

14 Different meanings

Look at the dictionary entry for the word *course*.

> **course** /kɔrs/ noun
>
> **1** [C] a course (in/on sth) a complete series of *lessons: I've enrolled in an English course.* ▪ *A course in self-defense.* **2** [C] one of the parts of a meal: *a three-course lunch* ▪ *I had chicken for the main course.* **3** [C] an area where golf is played or where certain types of race take place: *a golf course* ▪ *a racecourse* **4** [C] a course (of sth) a series of medical treatments: *The doctor put her on a course of radiation therapy.* **5** [C, U] the route or direction that sth, especially an airplane, ship, or river takes: *We changed course and sailed toward land.*

Match the word *course* in the sentences with a meaning 1–5 in the dictionary entry.

a I'm on a *course* of antibiotics. ___

b My daughter did a *course* in interior design. ___

c We had to run a five-mile cross-country *course*. ___

d A three-*course* meal consists of an appetizer, a main course, and a dessert. ___

e The road follows the *course* of the river. ___

Prepositions

15 Verb + preposition

1 Complete the sentences with a preposition from the box.

of	about	to	at	with	for	as	on

1 I think you're wrong. I don't agree _____ you at all.

2 You look worried. What are you thinking _____?

3 Look _____ that picture. Isn't it beautiful!

4 Are you listening _____ me?

5 If you have a problem, talk _____ the teacher.

6 **A** What were you and Alex talking _____?

 B Oh, this and that.

7 We might have a picnic tomorrow. It depends _____ the weather.

8 **A** What do you think _____ Pete?

 B I really like him.

9 Where's the cash register? I need to pay _____ this book.

10 **A** I lost your pen. Sorry.

 B It's all right. Don't worry _____ it.

11 **A** What are you looking _____?

 B My coat. Have you seen it?

12 Henry works _____ a taxi driver.

Listening

16 The world of work

1 🎧 Listen to an interview about Somali immigrants in Minneapolis, Minnesota. In which order (1–6) do you hear about the following?

☐ the types of programs that Ayan's organization offers

☐ why Somalis go to Minneapolis in particular

☐ Ayan's personal story of immigration

☐ problems that new Somali immigrants face

☐ the success of Somali businesses in Minnesota

☐ the weather in Minnesota

2 Now answer these questions.

1 When and why did Ayan's family leave Somalia?

2 Why do Somalis stay in Minnesota despite the cold weather?

3 What are some of the things that Somali immigrants have done to become successful?

4 Why are a lot of the newer Somali immigrants having a difficult time in Minnesota?

5 How is Ayan's organization trying to change the negative focus in the news and media?

3 Complete the extracts from the interview with the correct form of the verbs in parentheses.

---

1 We first _____ (arrive) in Hartford, Connecticut, but my parents _____ (have) a difficult time finding work there.

2 Minnesota's winters _____ (be) pretty difficult. It _____ (not seem) like the kind of place that people from a hot country like Somalia would like to live. _____ you and your family _____ (learn) to love the winter?

3 The Somali immigrant community _____ (be) successful in other ways, too. More and more young Somalis _____ (go) to college. The University of Minnesota's Somali Student Association _____ (have) over 500 members.

🎧 Listen again and check.

2 The work week

Simple Present and Present Continuous – active and passive • Adjectives that describe
character • Phrasal verb + noun • *-s* at the end of a word • States and activities

Present tenses

1 Recognizing tenses

Read the text. Use the present verb forms in
italics to complete the chart.

Simple Present (x 7)		
lives	*see*	*find.*
overlooks	*paint*	
paints	*walk*	

Present Continuous (x 6)		
is working	*is planning*	*are leaving*
is becoming.	*am painting.*	*is falling*

Simple Present passive (x 2)	
is inhabited.	
are employed	

Present Continuous passive (x 1)
is being developed.

AMERICAN ARTIST, BORN AND BRED

EMMA ANDERSON is one of the U.S.'s best up-and-coming artists.
HENRY LUCAS went to visit her at her home.

Emma Anderson was born in Ashville, North Carolina. She
studied at the University of North Carolina at Chapel Hill. She
lives in a small mountain town with her husband, Duncan, and
her three children. Home is a 100-year-old farmhouse which
overlooks the Great Smoky Mountains. Duncan is a writer and *is
working* on his new book.

Emma *paints* animals and wildlife. "I *paint* what I *see* around
me," she told me, "birds, animals, trees, and flowers. I *find* my
work totally absorbing. I *work* outside in the open air for as long
as it is light, from dawn until dusk – about 13 hours a day in the
summer, though less now because it's winter."

Her work *is becoming* increasingly popular, and she *is planning*
to open a gallery in her town. "Right now I *'m painting* a series of
wild flowers," she said to me over coffee in her studio.

The town *is inhabited* by 700 people who *are employed* mainly
in the tourism industry. The population *is falling* because young
people *are leaving* the town to look for work. The town *is being
developed* further as a tourist destination – 50,000 visitors come
every year – but it is big enough for Emma to escape and find
her inspiration. ∿

2 Producing tenses

Complete the sentences using the verb in the box and the tense given.

paint

1 SIMPLE PRESENT
Emma **paints** animals and wildlife.

2 PRESENT CONTINUOUS
Right now she _is painting_ a series of wild flowers.

find

3 SIMPLE PRESENT
She _finds_ her work totally absorbing.

4 SIMPLE PRESENT PASSIVE
A lot of birds _are found_ near her home.

think

5 PRESENT CONTINUOUS
Emma _is thinking_ of opening a small gallery.

6 SIMPLE PRESENT PASSIVE
She _is thought_ to be one of the U.S.'s best up-and-coming artists.

know

7 SIMPLE PRESENT PASSIVE
Her town _is known_ as a tourist destination.

8 SIMPLE PRESENT
People all over the U.S. _know_ her work.

work

9 SIMPLE PRESENT
She _works_ in the open air from dawn until dusk.

10 PRESENT CONTINUOUS
She _is_ only _working_ six hours today because it's winter.

3 Questions

Here are some answers to questions about Emma Anderson. Write the questions.

1 Where _does she live_ ?
In a small mountain town.

2 How many _children does she have_ ?
Three.

3 What _is her husband's job._ ?
He's a writer.

4 _What does she paint_ ?
Animals and wildlife.

5 Where _does she work_ ?
In the open air.

6 _What is she_ doing right now?
She's painting a series of wild flowers.

7 _Why are_ young people _leaving._ ?
Because there aren't any jobs.

8 _How many visitors come the town every year_ ?
50,000.

4 Negatives

Correct the information in these sentences.

1 Emma lives in Canada.
She doesn't live in Canada. She lives in the U.S.

2 Her husband is a farmer.
Her husband isn't a farmer. He's a writer.

3 Emma paints portraits.
Annie doesn't paint portraits. She paints animals and wildlife.

4 She's painting a series of wild birds.
_____

5 The people in the town are employed in farming.
She The people in the town aren't employed in farming. They are employed in the tourism industry

6 Young people are leaving the town to get married.
_____

Adverbs

5 Adverbs of time and frequency

Put the adverbs in parentheses in the correct place in the sentence. Some may go in more than one place.

1 I drink coffee.
(never / in the evenings)

I never drink coffee in the evenings.

2 How do you see Julie?
(often / these days)

How often do you see Julie these days?

3 I go to the movies.
(hardly ever / anymore)

I hardly ever go to the movies anymore.

4 I bump into my old girlfriend.
(from time to time)

I bump into my old girlfriend from time to time

5 Do you come here?
(often)

Do you come here often?

6 I don't cook. I eat out.
(much / usually)

I don't cook much. I usually eat out.

7 I see my grandparents.
(only / once a month)

I only see my grandparents once a month.

8 I wash my hair, and I have it cut.
(twice a week / every month)

I wash my hair twice a week, and I have it cut every month.

9 Children play on their own outdoors.
(rarely / nowadays)

Children rarely play on their own outdoors nowadays.

10 I spend commuting.
(three hours a day / sometimes)

Sometimes, I spend commuting three hours a day.

Pronunciation

6 -s at the end of a word

The pronunciation of -s at the end of a word can be /s/, /z/, or /ɪz/.

1 /s/ In these words, the final -s is pronounced /s/.

🎧 Listen and repeat.

pots	hits	parents	laughs	likes
stops	chefs	hates	months	wants

2 /z/ In these words, the final -s is pronounced /z/.

🎧 Listen and repeat.

friends	comes	has	eggs	goes
news	gives	does	sees	clothes
lessons	sings	travels	pens	moves

3 /ɪz/ In these words, the final -s is pronounced /ɪz/.

🎧 Listen and repeat.

nurses	washes	raises	watches
brushes	misses	switches	buses
challenges	places	wages	revises

4 Put these words into the correct column.

changes	surfs	bats	sells	buildings
loves	beaches	weeks	organizes	learns
sentences	wants	breathes	cooks	matches

/s/	/z/	/ɪz/
groups	**jobs**	**lunches**
cooks	buildings	changes
surfs	learns	beaches
weeks	loves	matches
wants		

🎧 Listen, check, and repeat.

▶▶ **Phonetic Symbols p. 93**

Simple Present and Present Continuous

7 Questions and negatives

Read the text and do the exercises.
Complete the questions in the Simple Present.

1 How fast _does the Bullet trains go_ ?
300 km/h (190 mph).

2 How many passengers _are carry on the trains_?
800.

3 How long _does the journey take_ ?
Two hours 48 minutes.

4 How much _money does Mogi earn_ ? _{kumiko}
125,000 yen ($1,050).

5 How many women _does Kumiko_ ?
1,300.

Complete Kumiko Mogi's questions in the Present Continuous.

6 What _are the passengers wearing_ ?

7 Who _are they travel with_ ?

8 How many bags _are they carry_ ?

9 What books or newspapers _are the reading_ ?

Write the negative sentences.

10 Mogi / not sell / ice cream / the winter.
Mogi doesn't sell any ice cream in the winter.

11 People / not want beef or rice / breakfast.
People don't want beef or rice for breakfast.

12 She / not have lemonade.
She doesn't have lemonade, yet.

13 The trolley girls / not sit down.
The trolley girls don't sit down.

14 Mogi / not turn / back towards / customers.
Mogi doesn't turn her back towards the customers.

15 She / not want / do a different job.
She doesn't want to do a different job.

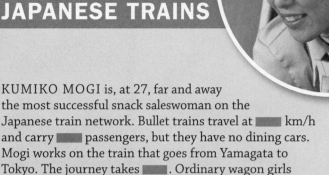

THE QUEEN OF FAST FOOD ON JAPANESE TRAINS

KUMIKO MOGI is, at 27, far and away the most successful snack saleswoman on the Japanese train network. Bullet trains travel at ▮▮▮ km/h and carry ▮▮▮▮ passengers, but they have no dining cars. Mogi works on the train that goes from Yamagata to Tokyo. The journey takes ▮▮▮▮. Ordinary wagon girls average about 25,000 yen ($210) on the six-hour return trip. Mogi earns ▮▮▮.

She is more successful than all her colleagues, and she is now an instructor to the ▮▮▮ women who work on the East Japan Railways bullet trains.

"The important thing in this job," she says, "is to know the customers. I size them up very carefully as they are getting on the train, and I ask myself these questions.

- What / the passengers / wear?
- Who / they / travel / with?
- How many bags / they / carry?
- What books or newspapers / they / read?"

Based on the answers, she decides what people will want to eat and drink. "If it's hot, I sell a lot of banana cakes and iced coffee for breakfast. No ice cream in the winter. People buy lunchboxes of beef and rice. I also have dried fish, salted beef tongue, and juice. But no lemonade."

No seats are provided for the trolley girls. They continue selling until the door opens at the terminal.

Unlike her competition, Mogi pulls her trolley, she doesn't push it. "I never turn my back towards the customers. I can look at their faces all the time and figure out what they want."

Does she want to get a promotion and do something different? "Of course not," she replies. "You can see that I'm perfect for this job."

States and activities

8 Simple Present or Present Continuous?

> **Remember the verbs that rarely take the continuous.**
>
> know hope want
> believe understand
> think suppose
> prefer love like
> mean care
> remember forget
>
> have belong
> own cost
> depend need
> owe matter
> contain consist

1 Complete the sentences with one of the verbs from the box.

have	consist	depend	~~belong~~	prefer
not matter	need	cost	smell	owe
hope	look	own	remember	not suit

1 This book **belongs** to me.
2 The U.S. _has_ a population of 321 million.
3 Water _consists_ of hydrogen and oxygen.
4 "I forgot your book again. Sorry."
   "It _not matter_ . You can bring it later."
   does
5 I _need_ a haircut. My hair is too long.
6 _Do_ you _own_ this apartment, or do you rent it?
7 Gasoline _costs_ about $2.80 a gallon.
8 I've borrowed so much money. How much do I _owe_ you?
9 You _look_ pretty. Where did you get that dress?
10 Congratulations on your wedding. I _hope_ you'll be very happy.
11 The sweater fits you very well, but the color _doesn't matter_ you.
   suit
12 We might have a picnic. It _depends_ on the weather.
13 I like both tea and coffee, but I _prefer_ tea.
14 You _smell_ nice. What perfume are you wearing?
15 I _remember_ when you were a little girl. You were very cute.

2 Complete the pairs of sentences. Use the verb in **bold** once in the Simple Present and once in the Present Continuous.

1 **come**

   Julian _comes_ from Peru.
   We _come_ on the ten o'clock train.

2 **not have**

   He _doesn't have_ any children.
   He _didn't haven_ breakfast this morning.
   isn't

3 **see**

   I _am seeing_ the dentist next week. I think I need
   will
   a filling.
   I _see_ what you mean, but I don't agree.

4 **not think**

   I have an exam tomorrow, but I _don't think_ about it.
   I _don't think_ she's very clever.

5 **watch**

   Be quiet. I _am watching_ my favorite TV show.
   I always _watch_ it on Thursday evenings.

6 **not enjoy**

   We _aren't enjoy_ this party at all. The music is too loud.
   We _don't enjoy_ big parties.

7 **use**

   This room _is_ usually _usezzag_ for
   used
   big meetings.
   But today it _is being used_ for a party.

Present passive

9 Recognizing tenses

Read the text. Find examples of the Simple Present and Present Continuous, active and passive, and complete the chart.

Simple Present active (x 3)
imports
exports
move

Present Continuous active (x 3)
is playing   is falling   are staying

Simple Present passive (x 6)
is based   are owned
are imported   are employed
is employed   are unemployed.

Present Continuous passive (x 1)
are being taxed

10 Office life

Put the verbs in parentheses in the Simple Present passive.

1 In 54% of offices, employees _are baned_ (ban) from using social networking sites such as Facebook.

2 40% of Internet use in the office _is doesn't related._ (not relate) to work.

3 Work hours _are_ often _used. using_ (use) to conduct personal business.

4 45% of work time _is wasted_ (waste) on chat, drinking coffee, and taking personal phone calls.

5 Open-plan offices _are disliked_ (dislike) by 40% of workers.

6 Team-bonding days _are despised_ (despise) by nearly everyone.

7 Most employees complain that they _are overworked_ (overwork) and _don't appreciated_ (not appreciate).

8 Many people _is stressing stressed_ (stress) by the number of e-mails they receive.

9 More than six trillion business e-mails _are sended_ (send) worldwide every year.

10 Stress at work _is associated_ (associate) with the risk of heart disease. It _also knowed is knew_ (also know) to cause depression.

■ The U.S. economy *is based* on the goods and services industries – insurance, banking, tourism, government, and retail. With globalization and the communications revolution, goods, services, and finance *move* freely and easily around the world, and this *is playing* a big part in changing the U.S.

■ The U.S. *exports* industrial supplies, motor vehicle parts, food, and beverages. It *imports* raw materials, cars, gas, and oil. Most of its electrical and electronic goods *are imported* from China, Canada, and Mexico. Only 17% of the working population *is employed* in manufacturing. 83% is employed in service-producing industries.

■ Many businesses in the public service sectors such as water, electricity and gas, railways, and airports, *are owned* privately.

■ Americans *are being taxed* at a local, state, and federal level. The proportion of time that Americans spend working *is falling*. Young people *are staying* longer in education. More women *are employed* than men. 6.5% of women *are unemployed*, compared to 7% of men.

Vocabulary

11 Adjectives that describe character

1 Match a description in **A** with an adjective in **B**.

A	B
1 **g** She likes being with people and is fun.	a̶ generous
2 **h** She always has to get everything she wants.	b̶ optimistic
3 **a** He always gives great presents.	c̶ kind
4 **c** She cares about people and wants to make them happy.	d̶ shy
5ᵀ **b** She wants to do really well in life.	e eccentric
6 **x** He only ever thinks of himself.	f̶ rude
7 **b** She always looks on the bright side of things.	g̶ sociable
8ᵀ **d** He hates meeting people and having to talk to them.	h̶ spoiled
9 e **e** She has some very strange ideas.	i̶ ambitious
10 **j** He never does any work at all.	j lazy
11 **k** You never know how he's going to be, happy or sad.	k̶ moody
12 **f** He always says things to upset and annoy people.	l̶ selfish

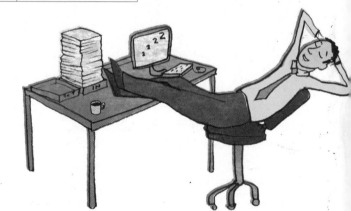

2 Match these adjectives with their opposites in exercise 1.

- x̶ **a** cheap
- 2 **j** hardworking
- 3 **l** unselfish
- 4 **k** cheerful
- 5 **e** confident
- 6 **d** antisocial
- 7 **f** polite
- 8 **c** unkind
- 9 **b** pessimistic
- 10 **i** unambitious

3 Complete the sentences with an adjective from exercise 2.

1 The Japanese have a reputation for being ___**polite**___ .

2 He's so ___unkind___ —he never buys anyone a drink.
   cheap

3 I'm afraid I'm pretty ___unselfish___ —I hate going to parties and making small talk. unambitious

4 She always thinks the worst is going to happen. She's very ___pessimistic___ .

5 He's so ___hardworking___ . He's always the first to arrive in the office and the last to leave.

6 She's totally ___antisocial___ . There's nothing in life she wants to do and nowhere she wants to go.

7 Jane's always happy and smiling. She's a ___cheerful___ person.

8 Parents have to be ___confident___ . Their children have to come first. unselfish

9 Henry's so sure about himself and what he can do. He's very ___unambitious___. confident

10 We have to invite Paula. It would be so ___cheap___ to invite her husband and not her. unkind

14   Unit 2 • The work week

Phrasal verbs

12 Phrasal verb + noun (1)

1 Many phrasal verbs go with a noun. Match a verb in **A** with a word or phrase in **B**.

A		B	
1	**b** turn on	a	clothes in a store
2	**f** look after	b	a light
3	**g** fill out	c	some information
4	**c** find out	d	your coat
5	**a** try on	e	the television at bedtime
6	**i** look up	f	your parents
7	**h** pick up	g	a form
8	**d** take off	h	something you dropped
9	**e** turn off	i	a word in the dictionary
10	**j** get along with	j	the baby

2 Complete the sentences with the correct form of the phrasal verbs in exercise 1.

1 **A** Can I ___try on___ these jeans, please?

   B Sure. The fitting rooms are over there.

2 I can't go out tonight. I'm _looking after_ ~~get along with~~ the children.

3 There's a show I want to watch. Can you ___turn ~~off~~ on___ the TV?

4 No one's watching the TV. ___Turn___ it ___off___, please.

5 **A** What do I do with this form?

   B Just ___fill___ it ___out___, and give it to the receptionist.

6 If there's a word I don't know, I ___look___ it ___up___ in my dictionary.

7 Please ___take off___ your dirty shoes before you come in.

8 I ~~look after~~ _get along with_ my sister but not my brother. We fight all the time.

9 Oh, no—I've dropped my purse. Could you ___pick___ it ___up___ for me? Thanks.

10 **A** Can you ___find out___ the time of the next train to New York?

   B OK. I'll look on the Internet.

Listening

13 What's cooking?

1 🎧 Listen to Matt Greenberg, a TV chef. He's cooking a recipe for "Bread and Butter Pudding." Put a check (✓) next to the ingredients he uses in the recipe.

- [✓] 12 slices white bread, cut into triangles
- [✓] 8 egg yolks
- [ ] 4 Tbs unsalted butter
- [ ] 1 tsp salt
- [✓] 2 cups sugar
- [✓] a few drops vanilla extract
- [ ] ½ cup raisins
- [ ] 1 lemon
- [✓] 2 cups milk
- [ ] 5 cups flour
- [✓] 2 cups heavy cream
- [✓] 1 orange rind (grated)

2 Are the sentences true (✓) or false (✗)?

✓ 1 Matt works in a hotel kitchen.

✗ 2 He doesn't like running a kitchen because it's so stressful.

✓✗ 3 Many people think that British cooking is a little boring.

✓ 4 The recipe he's making today isn't expensive.

✓✗ 5 He's making the recipe slightly differently today.

3 Complete the lines from the show with the correct form of the verb in parentheses.

1 You ___come___ (come) from England originally, don't you?

2 I ___think___ (think) simple traditional cooking with the best ingredients is never boring.

3 So what _are you making_ ~~you made~~ (you / make) for us today?

4 Now, I normally ___use___ (use) just raisins in this, but today I'm ___putting___ (put) some fresh orange in as well.

5 Right, now I ___am heating___ (heat) the milk, cream, and vanilla in a pan …

6 These are ___grown___ (grow) in the Mediterranean.

7 Mmm, just the way I ___like___ (like) it.

8 Well, they ___don't know___ (not know) what they ___are missing___ (miss), do they?

🎧 Listen again and check.

3 Good times, bad times

Simple Past and Past Continuous – active and passive • Past Perfect
• Prepositions of time • Birth, marriage, death • Phonetic symbols; consonants

Past tenses

1 Recognizing tenses

Read the text. Use the past verb forms in *italics*
to complete the chart.

Simple Past (x10)	
felt	wanted
bought	bought
paid	cost
~~wanted~~	made
wanted	put
~~went~~	
put	

Past Continuous (x3)
were visiting
was hanging
was standing

Simple Past passive (x4)
was pained
was sold
was repaired
was damaged

Past Perfect (x4)	
had damaged	had received
had decided	
had agreed	

Past Perfect Continuous (x1)
had been negotiating

Billionaire rips a hole in his Picasso worth millions

Steve Wynn, the billionaire art collector, *felt* extremely embarrassed after
he *had damaged* one of his own paintings by putting a hole in the canvas.

Wynn, the 107th richest man in America, runs hotels and casinos in Las
Vegas. He owns a Matisse, a Renoir, a Van Gogh, a Gauguin, and several
Warhols.

He *bought* a Picasso, *Le Rêve (The Dream)* in 1997. It *was painted* in 1932,
and it depicts Picasso's mistress as she is sitting daydreaming. Wynn *paid*
$48 million for it.

Despite being one of his favorite pictures, Wynn *had decided* to sell it. He
had been negotiating with an investor, Steven Cohen, and they *had agreed* on
a price of $139 million.

The weekend before the sale, some friends of his *were visiting* from New
York, staying in one of his hotels. They *wanted* to see the picture, which
was hanging in his office, before it *was sold*. Wynn *was standing* in front of
the picture and explaining its history when he accidentally *put* his elbow
through the canvas.

The picture *was repaired* by an art restorer in New York. It is now
impossible to see where it *was damaged*. Not surprisingly, Cohen no longer
wanted to buy it, so Wynn *put* it in a vault for safe keeping.

Years later, in 2013, Cohen finally *bought* the painting for $155 million,
$16 million more than the original price. Although Wynn *had received*
an insurance payment of $45 million after damaging the painting, the
restoration only *cost* him around $90,000. He certainly *made* quite a profit!

2 Producing tenses

Use information from the text to complete the sentences with the correct form of the verb in **bold**. Use each form once.

paint   SIMPLE PAST OR SIMPLE PAST PASSIVE?

1 Picasso _painted_ a picture of his mistress daydreaming.

2 *Le Rêve* _was painted_ in 1932.

visit   SIMPLE PAST OR PAST CONTINUOUS?

3 His New York friends ~~were visited~~ _were visiting_ for the weekend.

4 They often ~~visited~~ _visited_ ~~were visiting~~ him in Las Vegas.

see   SIMPLE PAST OR PAST PERFECT?

5 When his friends ~~had~~ _saw_ the Picasso, they were amazed.

6 When his friends _had saw seen_ the Picasso, they left the office.

put   SIMPLE PAST OR SIMPLE PAST PASSIVE?

7 He _put_ his elbow through the canvas.

8 *Le Rêve* _was put_ into a vault to keep it safe.

3 Questions

Write the questions.

1 **When did he buy the Picasso** ?
In 1997.

2 _When was it painted_ ?
In 1932.

3 _How much did Wynn pay for it the Picasso_ ?
$48 million.

4 _Where was it_ hanging?
In Wynn's office.

5 _How was it restored repaired by_ ?
By an art restorer in New York.

4 Negatives

Make these sentences negative.

1 *Le Rêve* was painted by Van Gogh.
It wasn't painted by Van Gogh.

2 Wynn's friends were staying in his house.
Wynn's friend weren't staying in his house

3 They had seen the Picasso before.
They hadn't seen the Picasso before.

4 Wynn kept the Picasso.
Wynn didn't kept the Picasso.

5 The damage lessened the painting's value.
The damage didn't lessened the painting's value

Simple Past and Past Continuous

5 *What was he doing? What did he do?*

Read the newspaper stories and answer the questions.

HERO SAVES MAN'S LIFE

Jim Wilson, 38, was driving home from work at around 6:30 in the evening when he saw a yellow VW van, driven by Carl Davidson, crash into a tree. Without thinking of his own safety, he pulled the young man out of the van and took him straight to the hospital. The doctors say Carl will make a complete recovery.

1 What was Jim Wilson doing when he saw the accident?
He was driving home from work.

2 What did he do when he saw the accident?
He pulled the young man out of the van and took him straight to the hospital.

Dog attacked in park by swans

Hilary Benting, 54, was taking her dog, Toby, for a walk in City Park last Thursday afternoon. She was throwing sticks into the pond for Toby to retrieve. He was swimming in the pond when he was attacked by two swans. He received cuts and bruises. Mrs. Benting called park officials to help, but there was little they could do.

3 What was Mrs. Benting doing when her dog was attacked? What was Toby doing?
She was throwing sticks into the pond for Toby to retrieve.

4 What did she do when her dog was attacked?
She called park officials to help, but there was little they could do.

Shock for bank customers

■ Customers in the Whitehall Savings Bank were shocked yesterday as they were standing in a line talking to each other. At 11:15 two masked robbers burst into the bank carrying shotguns. Sixty-year-old Martin Webb suffered a heart attack and was taken to the hospital. The robbers escaped with $800,000.

5 What was happening in the bank when the robbers burst in?
Talking to each other.

6 What happened to Martin Webb when the robbers burst in?
The robbers escaped with $800,000

Past Perfect

6 What had happened?

Complete the sentences. Use the prompts in parentheses and the Past Perfect.

1 I was broke because I <u>'d spent all my money on clothes</u>. (spend / money / clothes)

2 Jane was furious because she <u>'d overslept and missed the bus</u>. (oversleep / miss the bus)

3 Mary was very disappointed with her son. He <u>hadn't studied enough fail exams</u>. (not study enough / fail exams)

4 Before his accident, Peter <u>had been the best player on the team</u>. (be / best player / team)

5 I was nervous as I waited at the gate. I <u>never had flown before</u>. (never / fly / before)

6 Jack wanted a new challenge in his work. He <u>had been doing the same job for ten years</u>. (do / same job / ten years) (continuous)

7 Simple Past or Past Perfect?

(Circle) the correct tenses in the story.

A Busy Day

It was ten o'clock in the evening. Peter (1) (sat)/had sat down on his sofa and thought about the day. What a busy day it (2) was/(had been)! This was his first night in his own apartment. He (3) (lived)/had lived his whole life with his family, and now for the first time, he (4) (was)/had been on his own.

He sat surrounded by boxes that he (5) didn't manage/(hadn't managed) to unpack during the day. It (6) (took)/had taken months to get all his things together. His mother (7) was/(had been) very generous, buying him things like towels and mugs.

He (8) (went)/had gone into the kitchen and (9) (made)/had made a sandwich. He suddenly (10) (felt)/had felt very tired and yawned. No wonder he (11) (was)/had been tired! He (12) was/(had been) up since six o'clock in the morning. He (13) (decided)/had decided to eat his sandwich and go to bed. But he didn't make it. He sat down on his sofa, and before he knew it, he (14) (was)/had been fast asleep.

Tense review

8 ate, was eating, or had eaten?

Put the verb in **bold** in the Simple Past, Past Continuous, or Past Perfect.

eat

1 I couldn't understand what she was saying because she **was eating** an apple.

2 The meal was terrible, but John <u>ate</u> it all up. He must have been hungry.

3 There was nothing in the fridge. The kids <u>had eaten</u> everything.

talk

4 The class was so boring. The teacher just <u>talked</u> for a whole hour.

5 I knew about Annie's problem because I <u>talked</u> to her mother the day before.

6 Who <u>had/were</u> you <u>talked/talking</u> to on the phone just now?

drive

7 "How did you get here?" "I <u>had driven/drove</u>."

8 I was tired and needed to go to bed. I <u>drove/had driven</u> 300 miles that day.

9 I <u>had driven/was driving</u> to work when I had an accident and hit a tree.

Past passive

9 Simple Past passive

Put the verbs in parentheses in the Simple Past passive.

1 *Romeo and Juliet* **was written** (write) in 1595 or 1596.

2 It <u>was based</u> (base) on a traditional Italian tale.

3 It isn't known when it <u>was</u> first <u>performed</u> (perform).

4 The play <u>was published</u> (publish) in 1597.

5 Many of Shakespeare's plays <u>were performed</u> (perform) at the Globe Theatre in London.

6 The original theater <u>was built</u> (build) in 1599.

7 The theater <u>was destroyed</u> (destroy) by fire in 1613.

8 The 1996 movie version, starring Leonardo di Caprio, <u>were aimed</u> (aim) at a younger audience.

9 The movie <u>was shot</u> (shoot) in Mexico City.

10 The musical and movie *West Side Story* <u>was inspired</u> (inspire) by Shakespeare's play.

Love on the subway

10 Questions and negatives

Read the first online article.
Complete the questions.

1 When <u>was she visiting Boston</u> ?
  Last weekend.

2 Who <u>was she looking at</u> ?
  A young commuter.

3 What <u>was she doing</u> doing?
  Looking out the window.

4 Why <u>was she not talk to him</u> ?
  Because she was too shy.

5 Which train <u>was right the man traveling on</u> ?
  The E train.

6 Where <u>did the man get off at about</u> ?
  At Huntington Avenue.   <u>2:30 p.m.</u>

Read the second article.
Complete the negative sentences.

7 She / not see / the man since last weekend.
  She hadn't seen the man since last weekend.

8 She / not receive / any replies on the Internet.
  <u>She hadn't received any replies on the Internet.</u>

9 Mr. Wellikoff / not sit / on the subway.
  <u>Mr. Wellikoff hadn't sit on the subway.</u>   *(didn't)*

10 He / not use / Facebook or Instagram all week.
  <u>He hadn't used Facebook or Instagram all week.</u>

11 He / not know / why people were looking at him.
  <u>He couldn't know why people were looking at him.</u>

12 Mr. Wellikoff / not date / anyone.
  <u>Mr. Wellikoff hadn't dated anyone.</u>
            wasn't

Read the third article.
Complete the text using the verbs from the box.

got	went	~~met~~
had	enjoyed	~~did~~
was looking	had invited	

THURSDAY, JANUARY 11

Girl looks for love on the subway

Mireille Gaudreau was visiting Boston last (1) ▮▮▮ when she saw (2) ▮▮▮ on the subway. He was (3) ▮▮▮. She didn't talk to him because (4) ▮▮▮. However, she *did* take his photograph on her cell phone. She went back to Montreal but couldn't forget the handsome man she'd seen on the subway, so she posted his photo and a message on Instagram, Facebook, and Twitter in hopes that someone would recognize him.

The mystery man was traveling on the (5) ▮▮▮ train and got off at (6) ▮▮▮ at about 2:30 p.m.

■ If you know the man, or are him, post a comment below or send a private message to the *Daily Click* **here**.

The mystery man

FRIDAY, JANUARY 12

Tourist finds her mystery man

The Daily Click has ended the love search of a Canadian tourist. Mireille Gaudreau had been looking for a young man she'd seen last weekend on the Boston subway.

Mireille posted his photo on the Internet, but no one replied. We posted his picture yesterday, and he was identified as Sam Wellikoff, an art student from Brookline. His classmate contacted *The Daily Click*.

Mr. Wellikoff said, "I hadn't seen the photo. I hadn't been on Facebook or Instagram in a few days, and I don't use Twitter. I couldn't understand why people were giving me funny looks when I got to class this morning."

Miss Gaudreau was very pleased to learn that Mr. Wellikoff didn't have a girlfriend.

Mireille Gaudreau in Montreal yesterday

WEDNESDAY, FEBRUARY 7

Couple delighted with first date

The couple who (13) <u>had</u> after an international search on the Internet have had their first date in Boston. Mireille Gaudreau, 25, took the bus back from Montreal this past weekend after finding Sam Wellikoff, 28.

The couple (14) <u>enjoyed</u> *did* a sightseeing tour of Boston and then (15) <u>had enjoyed</u> lunch in the North End.

Mr. Wellikoff said, "It (16) <u>went</u> very well. We had a lot of fun, and we really (17) <u>enj</u> ourselves. We (18) <u>got</u> along really well."   *enjoyed*

Miss Gaudreau said that she (19) <u>had invited</u> Sam to go to Montreal in a couple of weeks, and that she (20) <u>was looking</u> forward to showing him her hometown.

Vocabulary

11 Birth, marriage, and death

> **!** 1 The verb *marry* is used without a preposition.
> *My sister **married** a plumber.*
>
> 2 *Get married* refers to the change of state between being single and being married.
> *We **got married** in 2002.*
>
> 3 *Married* refers to the state.
> *Is your brother **married**?*
>
> 4 *Get married* and *be married* can both be used with the preposition *to*.
> *She **got married to** Gary last weekend.*
> *My sister **is married to** a really nice guy.*

1 Complete the sentences with a word from the box.

birth	birthday	born

1 Where were you _____ ?
2 When is your _____ ?
3 She gave _____ to a beautiful healthy boy.
4 (*On an official form*) Date of _____
5 Congratulations on the _____ of little Albert.
6 What are you doing for your _____ this year?

2 Complete the sentences with the words from the box.

get married	marry	married	got married
been married	wedding	marriage	

1 **A** Are you _____ ?
   B No, I'm single. But I'd like to _____ someday.
2 Darling, I love you. Will you _____ me?
3 How many times has she _____ ?
4 We're engaged, and we're going to _____ next fall.
5 My wife and I have _____ for twenty-five years.
6 We had a lovely _____ in a small country inn.
7 Did you hear? James and Sue _____ last week.
8 Their _____ was always perfect until the end.

3 Complete the sentences with a word from the box.

dying	dead	died	death	die

1 Shakespeare _____ in 1616.
2 Julius Caesar was stabbed to _____ by his best friend, Brutus.
3 **A** Is old Bertie Harrison still alive?
   B I'm sure he's _____. Didn't he _____ a few years ago?
4 Her father's _____ came as a great shock. He _____ of a heart attack.
5 She screamed when she saw the _____ mouse on the floor.
6 Our poor old cat is _____. We've had her for fifteen years. She just sleeps all day long.
7 Every winter thousands of birds _____ in the cold weather.
8 Those flowers have _____. Throw them away.

Prepositions

12 *in / at / on* for time

Complete the sentences with *in, at, on,* or – (no preposition).

1 **A** What did you do ____ last weekend?

   B ____ Friday night we went to a party. We slept late ____ Saturday morning, and then ____ the afternoon we went shopping. ____ seven o'clock some friends came over for dinner. We didn't do much ____ Sunday—____ the evening we just watched TV. What about you?

2 I'll call you ____ next week ____ Thursday. It'll probably be ____ the afternoon ____ about 3:00 p.m. OK?

3 I don't see my parents much. ____ Thanksgiving Day, usually, and ____ the summer.

4 ____ November 9th, 1989, the Berlin Wall was opened. For the first time ____ the late twentieth century Germans could go from West to East Berlin without travel restrictions.

5 **A** You look tired. What were you doing ____ last night?

   B I was trying to finish my History essay. I'm having to work a lot ____ night lately. It has to be handed in ____ this Friday, and I still have a lot to write.

   A Oh well, I'll see you ____ lunchtime—if you're still awake.

6 The weather in New York is unreliable. ____ summer it can be very hot, but it often rains ____ April and June. The summer was awful ____ last year. The best weather is usually ____ spring and fall.

❗

1 We use *at* for times and certain expressions.
   at 8:00
   at midnight
   at lunchtime
   at the moment

2 We use *on* for days and dates.
   on Friday
   on Friday morning
   on September 12th
   on Saturday evening

3 We use *in* for longer periods such as months, seasons, and years.
   in April
   in 2002
   in the summer
   in the nineteenth century

4 We also use *in* for parts of the day.
   in the morning
   in the afternoon
   in the evening (but **at** night)

5 There is no preposition before *last, next, this,* or *tomorrow.*
   Did you go out **last** night?
   We're going away **this** weekend.
   I'll see you **next** week.
   Can you call me **tomorrow** morning?

Pronunciation

13 Phonetic symbols – consonants

1 Many phonetic symbols for consonants are easy.

/b/	/k/	/r/	/d/
/bɪɡ/ big	/kæn/ can	/rʌn/ run	/du/ do

/l/	/s/	/y/	
/lɪv/ live	/sɪt/ sit	/yes/ yes	

🎧 Listen and repeat.

2 These symbols are less obvious.

/θ/	/ð/	/ʃ/	/ʒ/
/θɪŋk/ think	/ðouz/ those	/ʃʊd/ should	/tɛləvɪʒn/ television/

/tʃ/	/dʒ/	/ŋ/	
/wɑtʃ/ watch	/dʒʌst/ just	/brɪŋ/ bring	

🎧 Listen and repeat.

3 Write the words in the correct box according to the sound underlined.

thought	tongue	this	age	machine
bath	mature	lunch	share	measure
weather	bank	gadget	pleasure	mother
fetch	thanks	German	wash	hang
revision				

/θ/	/tʃ/	/ʃ/
_____	_____	_____
_____	_____	_____
_____	_____	_____

/ð/	/dʒ/	/ʒ/
_____	_____	_____
_____	_____	_____
_____	_____	_____

/ŋ/		
_____		
_____		
_____		

🎧 Listen, check, and repeat.

▶▶ **Phonetic Symbols p. 93**

Listening

14 Memories

1 🎧 Listen to three friends, Carol, Anne, and Richard, talking about their earliest memories.

What is each person's earliest memory?

Carol _____

Anne _____

Richard _____

2 Answer the questions.

1 Why did Carol love sitting on her father's shoulders?
2 Why didn't her father want to carry her on the day she remembers?
3 Why is this memory so important in her life?
4 How does Anne know that she didn't invent her memory?
5 How long was it before her family used the Christmas tree the second time?
6 What does Carol think Anne's memory shows?

3 🎧 Listen again and complete the extracts from the conversation.

1 My mom says my dad _____ me a lot on his shoulders at that age, and I absolutely _____ it because he _____ a really big, tall man.

2 That's of this one day when I _____ with my mom and dad, and older sister. We _____ through some fields near where we _____ , and my dad _____ pick me up.

3 Well I know this isn't something _____ because when I _____ my mom, she _____ like that.

4 Getting it right

Modal and related verbs – obligation (*must, have to, should*);
permission (*can, allowed, to*) • Phrasal verbs – separable or inseparable?

Modal and related verbs

1 Recognizing verb forms

Read the text. Use the verb forms in italics to complete the chart.

Things that are IMPORTANT to do	
with *have to*	have to buy
with *must*	

Things that are IMPORTANT NOT to do	
with *shouldn't*	

Things that are NOT NECESSARY to do	
with *don't have to*	

Things that are A GOOD IDEA to do	
with *should*	

Things that you are ABLE or PERMITTED to do	
with *can*	

Things that are IMPOSSIBLE or FORBIDDEN to do	
with *can't*	
with *not allowed to*	

Tips for visitors to the U.S.

The weather You *should check* the weather before you come. The weather varies from region to region.

Food and drink In most coffee shops you *have to buy* your drink at the counter, then carry your drink to a table. You are usually served at a table in a nice cafe or restaurant.

Tipping is a problem. You *don't have to leave* a tip in a coffee shop, but in a restaurant you *should leave* about 15-20%. Similarly you *can tip* a taxi driver if you want.

In a restaurant, you *shouldn't say* "Give me the menu!" or "I want some water!" This is considered very rude. You *should be* polite and say "Could I have the menu, please." We tend to say "Please" and "Thank you" a lot.

People You *shouldn't address* people as "Mr." or "Mrs." We usually say: "Good morning," not "Good morning, Mr."

Transportation Obviously, you *have to have* a driver's license to rent a car, and the law says you *must wear* a seat belt in the back seat as well as the front. In some states, you *aren't allowed to use* your cell phone while driving.

Tourism The U.S. is a big country! You *can see* many different types of cities and landscapes, but you *can't do* it all in one trip. You *should choose* one region to explore — for example, Miami and the Florida keys, or Las Vegas and the Grand Canyon.

In rural areas, you may *have to rent* a car to get around, but in most cities, you *can get around* on the subway or other public transportation.

You *should research* the city or region before you visit to maximize your experience.

General You *can get* cash from ATM machines, which are everywhere.

You *aren't allowed to smoke* in any public buildings. You *can't smoke* in restaurants.

Obligation

2 *have to/don't have to*

Look at the photos. Match the sentences with the people.

1 [b] I have to wear business casual attire.
2 ☐ I always have to be home before 11:00 P.M.
3 ☐ My dad usually has to work in the evenings.
4 ☐ I don't have to get up at 6:30 A.M. anymore.
5 ☐ My husband has to take our children to school every morning.
6 ☐ My wife has to go to the hospital every week.
7 ☐ I have to get good grades this semester.
8 ☐ My little sister doesn't have to help with the housework.
9 ☐ I often have to travel abroad.

3 Questions with *have to*

Write the questions for these answers.

1 Why **does she have to** wear business casual attire?
   Because she has to meet a lot of important people.

2 Why _____ be home before 11:00 P.M.?
   Because his parents say that he has to.

3 Why _____ work in the evenings?
   Because he's a teacher, and he has to prepare lessons.

4 Why _____ get up at 6:30 A.M.?
   Because he's retired.

5 Why _____ go to the hospital?
   Because she broke her arm, and she has to have physiotherapy.

6 Why _____ get good grades this semester?
   Because he wants to go to Princeton University.

7 Why _____ help with the housework?
   Because her mother says that she is still too young.

8 Why _____ travel abroad?
   Because she works for an international company.

4 Forms of *have to*

Match a line in **A** with a line in **B**.

A
1 ☐ I don't have to get up early tomorrow …
2 ☐ My grandmother had to go to work …
3 ☐ We're having to economize …
4 ☐ You'll have to study hard …
5 ☐ You didn't have to buy me a present, …
6 ☐ Will I have to take the exam again …

B
a if you want to be a doctor.
b because it's the weekend.
c if I don't pass?
d when she was just 12.
e because we're saving up for a vacation.
f but it was very kind of you.

5 *must* and *have to*

> ❗ There is a difference between *must* and *have to*.
> *Must* expresses the authority of the speaker.
> *Have to* refers to the authority of another person, or to obligation generally.
> If you are not sure which one to use to express obligation, use *have to*.

Match the pairs of sentences with their meaning.

1 I must have a drink of water. [b]
   I have to drink lots of water. [a]
   a The doctor told me to.
   b I'm really thirsty.

2 I must do my homework tonight. ☐
   I have to do my homework tonight. ☐
   c I'm telling myself it's important.
   d That's why I can't come out with you tonight.

3 We must go to Paris some time. ☐
   We have to go to Paris next week. ☐
   e Another boring business trip! Yawn!
   f It would be so romantic!

4 I must water the plants today. ☐
   I have to water the plants today. ☐
   g I haven't watered them in days.
   h They need lots and lots of water.

5 We must have lunch soon. ☐
   We have to have lunch with our boss. ☐
   i What about next Wednesday?
   j We better look sharp!

6 Talking about obligation

Complete the sentences with *must*, *have to*, or *had to*.

a "You _____ be home by 11:00."

b "Bye! Dad said I _____ be home by 11:00."

a "You _____ stay in bed for a few days."

b "The doctor told me I _____ stay in bed for a few days."

a "I _____ wash my hair tonight."

b "I _____ wash all these dishes."

a "I _____ go and see the doctor."

b "Sorry, I _____ go to the doctor at 3 P.M."

7 *shouldn't / don't have to / didn't have to*

Choose the correct verb form.

1 We have a lot to do tomorrow. You *shouldn't / don't have to* go out tonight.

2 You *shouldn't / don't have to* tell Mary what I told you. It's a secret.

3 The museum is free. You *shouldn't / don't have to* pay to get in.

4 In the 19th century children *shouldn't / didn't have to* attend school up to the age of 16.

5 Terry's a millionaire. He *shouldn't / doesn't have to* go to work.

6 When I was a child I *didn't have to / don't have to* do my dishes. My mother did it for me.

7 We *shouldn't / don't have to* rush. We have plenty of time.

8 You *shouldn't / don't have to* play with knives. They're dangerous.

9 This is my favorite pen. You can borrow it, but you *shouldn't / don't have to* lose it.

10 **A** Should I come with you?

  B You can if you want, but you *shouldn't / don't have to*.

8 *should* for advice

1 Read the sentences. Give advice using *should* and an idea from the box.

do more exercise	~~let him play for an hour~~
take up a sport or a hobby	get it serviced

1 My son never wants to go out, he just plays computer games all day!

You <u>should let him play for an hour</u>, and then tell him to stop and do something else.

2 My car keeps breaking down.

_____ .

3 My wife isn't sleeping very well these days.

_____ .

4 Since he retired, my father doesn't know what to do with himself.

_____ .

2 Complete the questions with *do you think I should …?* and an idea from the box.

go to	~~go out with~~	say	take	have

1 Peter wants to go out with me. He's nice, but I only like him as a friend.

<u>**Do you think I should go out with**</u> him?

2 I've been offered admission to Columbia and Harvard.

Which university _____ ?

3 Everything on the menu looks wonderful!

What _____ ?

4 I have a terrible headache, and I can't read the instructions on this aspirin bottle.

How many _____ ?

5 My aunt has invited me to her picnic, but I don't want to go.

What _____ to her?

9 Modern manners

Do the quiz to see if you know how to behave!

Do **you** have good manners?

Choose the response that's true for you.

1 You're in a restaurant with friends and your cell phone rings. Should you …
   a answer it in front of them?
   b turn your phone off, of course?

2 You get a present for your birthday. You need to say thank you. Should you …
   a text?
   b e-mail?

3 You are at the dinner table. Your meal has arrived, but no one else's has. Should you …
   a start eating?
   b wait for everyone else to be served?

4 You've been invited to dinner. Should you take …
   a homemade baked goods?
   b something to offer — some flowers, a box of chocolates?

5 You get an invitation to the kind of evening you really can't stand. Should you …
   a ignore the invitation?
   b make up an excuse?

6 Your friend asks if you like his/her new clothes. You think they're awful. Should you …
   a tell the truth?
   b say they look great?

7 You're at home watching your favorite TV show when some friends arrive. Should you …
   a invite your friends to watch with you?
   b turn off the TV?

8 You're on the bus listening to your MP3 player. Someone asks you to turn it down. Should you …
   a pay no attention and carry on listening?
   b apologize and turn it down?

Of course it's impossible to say what is the correct way to behave in all situations. The more polite answers are probably **b**, the more impolite **a**.

1 Young people think it's OK to leave their phones on. Older people find this very rude.

2 An e-mail saying thank you is probably fine.

3 **a** is very impolite.

4 Either is fine.

5 **b** is probably what most people do if they really don't want to go.

6 It depends how well you know your friend.

7 Some people have no hesitation in keeping on the TV. For others this is incredibly rude.

8 **b** is the polite thing to do.

Permission and ability

10 *can* and *be allowed to*

Who says these sentences? Where?

1 "You can't park here. I'll have to give you a parking ticket."
   A police officer in the street.

2 "I'm sorry, sir, but you can't get on the plane without a passport."
   _____

3 "You aren't allowed to look at your notes during the exam."
   _____

4 "Shh! You can't talk in here. People are studying."
   _____

5 "You can take your seat belt off now. You still aren't allowed to use personal computers or cell phones."
   _____

6 "We're allowed to make one phone call a week, and we can go to the library, but we spend most of our time in our cells."
   _____

7 "You can take photographs, but you can't use flash or touch any of the exhibits."
   _____

8 "You aren't allowed to jump into the pool, but you can use the diving board at the deep end."
   _____

Obligation and permission

11 The pain and pleasure of being a teenager

Complete the interview with Ana and Ben with the correct form of *can*, *be allowed to*, or *have to*.

Interviewer What are some of the good things about being a teenager and not an adult?

Ana Well, we (1) _____ earn a living for a start.

Ben We (2) _____ go out with our friends, go shopping, go to the movies.

I So what you're saying is, what's good is that you have no responsibilities?

A Yeah, we're pretty free. We (3) _____ do what we like, most of the time.

B But money's a problem. What's good is that you (4) _____ pay bills, but it also means we can't buy what we want.

A Yes, we never have enough money.

I What do you think it's like being an adult?

A Well, adults have to worry about bills so they (5) _____ earn a living. They don't have as much free time as we do. They're always busy. They (6) _____ do what they want, when they want.

I Who do you feel more sorry for, your mom or your dad?

B My mom. She takes care of us kids, takes us to school and swimming and dance, and she goes to work. And she (7) _____ cook, clean, and run the house.

A I feel more sorry for my dad. He (8) _____ travel a lot, so we go weeks without seeing him, *and* that's really tough on him and us.

B But the very worst thing about being a teenager is that we have to go to school.

I Is that so bad?

A Yes! The rules are so stupid! There are certain clothes we (9) _____ wear, like short skirts or ripped jeans.

I What's so bad? I (10) _____ wear an ugly uniform when I was at school!

B And you (11) _____ do so much homework.

A And you can't skip class and (12) you _____ use your cell phone!

I Oh! What a difficult life you two lead!

Phrasal verbs

12 Separable or inseparable?

1 Put the noun in parentheses in two places in these sentences.

1 Could you turn / off (the light)?
   __Could you turn the light off?__   __Could you turn off the light?__

2 Look at the trash on the street! I have to pick / up (those empty bottles)!
   _____
   _____

3 I saw some beautiful clothes today. I tried / on (a coat), but I didn't buy it.
   _____
   _____

4 Please don't throw / away (those newspapers). I haven't read them yet.
   _____
   _____

5 I'll sort / out (this problem). Don't you worry about it.
   _____
   _____

2 Rewrite the sentences in the exercise above with the noun as a pronoun.

1 __Could you turn it off?__   4 _____
2 __I have to pick them up.__   5 _____
3 _____

3 Put the nouns in parentheses in just one place in these sentences.

1 I'm looking for (Peter – him).
   __I'm looking for Peter.__   __I'm looking for him.__

2 When you get to the reception, ask for (Mr. Smith – me).
   _____
   _____

3 I'm looking forward to (the party – it).
   _____
   _____

4 You go out tonight. I'll look after (the children – them).
   _____
   _____

5 I like my husband's family. I get along well with (my mother-in-law – her).
   _____
   _____

Listening

13 A radio call-in

1 Listen to a radio call-in about "rules that were made to be broken." There are three topics discussed:

| **a** Table manners | **b** School rules | **c** Driving rules |

Which topics do you think these lines from the call-in refer to? Put a, b, or c.

1 [a] You shouldn't put your elbows on the table.
2 [ ] … you have to have some way of showing responsibility.
3 [ ] They're saying you shouldn't eat at the wheel, aren't they?
4 [ ] Why aren't I allowed to leave school to have lunch?
5 [ ] Apparently you shouldn't read a map or talk to a passenger.
6 [ ] … you have to eat up everything on your plate.

🎧 Listen and check.

2 Choose the correct answer.

1 Tony thinks you can eat more *quickly / easily* with your elbows on the table.
2 He says we teach children to eat *too quickly / too much*.
3 Sarah wants to *stay in / leave* school to have lunch.
4 She thinks *older / younger* students should be allowed to leave school if they want to.
5 Andy explains that it's only *using a cell phone / eating at the wheel* that's actually illegal.
6 He thinks that paying attention to pets while driving is *less / more* dangerous than talking to someone.

3 Complete these lines from the call-in with the correct form of the phrasal verb from the box.

| come up to | cut off | get through | pick up |

1 "And it's just _____ ten minutes past nine."
2 "I think people just _____ these rules from their parents."
3 "Can you hear me? Oh, I'm sorry, it looks like Sarah's been _____ ."
4 "… do try calling again if you don't _____ the first time."

🎧 Listen again and check.

Vocabulary Crossword 1

Use the clues to complete the crossword. All these words and expressions have appeared in Units 1–4.

ACROSS

4 Juliet was very _____ when she heard Romeo's family name. (5)
6 The number of people living in a country is the _____. (10)
8 A _____ is someone who doesn't eat meat. (10)
10 Most of the world's _____ comes from the United States, Saudi Arabia, and Russia. (3)
13 Her health has picked up since she moved to a country with a sunny _____. (7)
14 When something is _____, it's very, very old. (7)
15 The _____ for Boniface's apartment is $45 a month. (4)
16 Someone who is no longer married is _____. (8)
19 In the U.S. you have to be 18 years old to _____ military service. (2)
20 My aunt lives in a _____ house (big). (5)
21 A _____ is someone who looks after people in a hospital. (5)
24 "What's the telephone area _____ for New York?" "It's 212." (4)
25 _____ is another word for "frightening." (5)
27 The Qu family motto is "save money, live simply, care _____ your friends." (3)
28 That building is _____! (4)
31 Joaquim is here _____ a business trip. (2)
32 A _____ is a very bad or frightening dream. (9)
33 You have to wear a seat _____ when you're driving. (4)

DOWN

1 Someone or something from a different country is _____. (7)
2 People once believed the earth was _____. (4)
3 The _____ of *Romeo and Juliet* has a very sad ending. (5)
4 Romeo went to the Capulet's party _____ (without an invitation). (9)
5 "I guess he's married." "I think _____ too." (I agree). (2)
7 If something is against the law, it is _____. (7)
9 Mmm! Are these potatoes fried, or _____ in the oven? (7)
11 How long does _____ take you to get to school? (2)
12 Someone who can speak two languages is _____. (9)
15 An HR manager has to _____ new staff. (7)

17 I _____ out of gas on the way home! I had to walk to the garage. (3)
18 I'm very _____ about soccer (have strong feelings about.) (10)
22 If you act very strangely and differently from other people, they think you are _____. (9)
23 That's the Manager, and that's her _____ Assistant, answering her calls. (8)
26 I was very _____ when I moved to Canada. (5)
29 We're just having dinner. Have you _____ yet? (5)
30 The people in a close-_____ family have strong relationships with each other. (4)

5 Our changing world

Future forms • Prepositions – adjective + prepositions •
Modal auxiliary verbs – *may, might, could*

Future forms

1 Recognizing tenses

Read the text. Use the future verb forms in *italics* to complete the chart.

prediction with *will* (x3) prediction with *won't* (x1)
will farm
prediction with *going to* (x2) intention/plan with (not) *going to* (x2)
arrangement with someone –   Present Continuous (x1)
possibility with *may* (x2)
possibility with *might* (x3)
possibility with *could* (x3)

IS IT THE END FOR MANY CALIFORNIAN FARMERS?

Like many other farmers in California, rice farmer Mike DeWit is facing huge problems caused by the severe droughts of the past few years. This year, because of water restrictions, DeWit *will farm* less than 40% of the fields he farmed two years ago. This means he *'s not going to rent* another tractor, he *'s not hiring* a driver, and he *'s not going to buy* as much fertilizer. In short, DeWit *won't produce* as much rice to be processed and sold and he *is going to lose* money, and his reduced crop *is going to have* a disastrous effect on other people in the industry.

Overall, the University of California, Davis estimates that the California farming industry *will lose* $2.7 billion and over 18,000 jobs this year alone. Next year *might prove* to be worse.

Climate scientists predict more trouble in the future: rising temperatures *will result* in drier land and longer, more severe droughts. This *may lead* to crop shortages, which *could cause* food prices to rise. If greenhouse gas emissions are not controlled, California *could experience* a "megadrought" – a drought far worse than any the U.S. has ever seen.

It's hard to be optimistic in the face of such predictions, but many California farmers, and scientists, remain hopeful. New technology *could help* farmers conserve and use water more efficiently in the future. Some believe that hydroponics – growing plants in water in greenhouses, which uses ten times less water than growing them in a field – *might offer* a solution to the problem.

Whatever the solution *might be*, if farmers don't find it soon, the U.S. *may face* a food crisis of epic proportions in just a few years.

will

2 Predictions

Write the sentences with *will* and the prompts.

1 You've been studying so hard.
I / sure / you / pass / exam.
I'm sure you'll pass your exam.

2 I think / go / bed soon. I have to be up early tomorrow.

_____

3 You don't need your umbrella. I / not / think / it / rain today.

_____

4 I'm going to an elegant restaurant tonight. I wonder if / I / meet anyone famous.

_____

5 You could ask Jack for some money, but I / not / think / he / lend you any.

_____

6 Are you seeing that new movie tonight?
I / sure / you / not / like it. It's very violent.

_____

7 I'll have some soup ready for you. I expect you / be / hungry after your trip.

_____

8 It's a good idea, but I / not think / it / work.

_____

3 Questions and negatives

Write the questions with *will* and the prompts in parentheses.

1 So you're going on vacation! (When / back?)
When will you be back?

2 So you finished your exams. (When / results?)

_____

3 So you ran out of money! (How / pay bills?)

_____

4 So you're going to live on an island! (What / eat?)

_____

5 So Peter's giving you a ride to the party! (How / home?)

_____

Complete the negatives with *won't* to express the same idea.

6 I'll pass.
I won't fail.

7 They'll arrive on time.
_____ be late.

8 He'll remember your birthday.

_____

9 You'll hate the movie.
_____ enjoy the movie.

10 Brazil will win the game.

_____

4 Offering to help

Make offers with *I'll*.

1 It's so hot in here!
I'll open the window.

2 I'm so thirsty.

_____

3 There's someone at the door.

_____

4 I don't have any money.

_____

5 I can't do the homework.

_____

going to

5 What's going to happen?

Look at the pictures. Write what is going to happen.

He's going to get a haircut.

_____

_____

_____

_____

_____

will or going to?

6 Planned or spontaneous?

Complete the conversations with *will* or *going to* and the verb in parentheses. Use the most natural form.

1 **A** Why are you wearing your old clothes?

   B Because I __'m going to wash__ (wash) the car.

2 **A** I have a headache. Do you have any aspirin?

   B Yes, they're in the bathroom. I _____ (get) some for you.

3 **A** Don't forget to tell me if I can help you.

   B Thank you. I _____ (give) you a call if I think of anything.

4 **A** Why are you making sandwiches?

   B Because we _____ (have) a picnic on the beach.

   A What a great idea! I _____ (get) the towels and the swimsuits.

5 **A** I'm going now! Bye!

   B Bye! What time _____ you _____ (be) back tonight?

   A I don't know. I _____ (call) you later.

6 **A** You still have my book. Did you forget?

   B I'm sorry. Yes, I forgot. I _____ (give) it back to you tomorrow.

7 **A** Dad, can you lend me $10, please? I _____ (give) it back tomorrow.

   B I don't know. What _____ you _____ (do)?

   A I _____ (see) a movie with Tina and Mike.

8 **A** Your exams start in two weeks. When _____ you _____ (start) studying? You haven't started studying yet.

   B I know. I _____ (study) tonight.

   A You're going out tonight.

   B I _____ (start) tomorrow night, then.

Present Continuous

7 Making arrangements

Complete the conversation with the Present Continuous form of the verbs in the box.

invite	come	~~have~~	make	stay
get	bring	give	travel	deliver

A Can you keep a secret?

B Yes, of course. What is it?

A (1) **I'm having** a surprise party for Rosa next Saturday. It's her thirtieth birthday.

B A surprise party! That'll be difficult to arrange without her knowing. Who (2) _____ you _____?

A Everybody. All our friends, her friends from work, all her family, even two aunts from Mexico. They (3) _____ up on Friday evening and they (4) _____ with cousins.

B What about the food and drinks? Where (5) _____ you _____ that from?

A It's all arranged. Marcello's restaurant (6) _____ all kinds of food on Saturday afternoon, and their chef (7) _____ even _____ a special birthday cake with pink icing and sugar flowers.

B Excellent! And what (8) _____ you _____ Rosa for her birthday? Did you get her a good present?

A Oh yes! I booked a very special vacation. A week for two in Bali! We (9) _____ first class, and we (10) _____ in a five-star hotel.

B That's a great idea. Very nice! I can see that you're going to enjoy her birthday, too! Am I invited to this party?

A Of course. But keep it a secret!

🎧 Listen and check.

Expressing the future

8 *will, going to,* or the Present Continuous?

Choose the correct form of the verb.

1 **A** Do you have a toothache again?
   B Oooh! It's agony! But I *see* / *'m seeing* the dentist this afternoon.

2 **A** Have you booked your vacation?
   B Yes, we have. We*'re going* / *'ll go* to Thailand.

3 **A** What a beautiful day! Not a cloud in the sky!
   B But the weather forecast says it*'s raining* / *'s going to rain.*

4 **A** Please don't tell anyone. It's a secret.
   B Don't worry. We *won't tell* / *'re not telling* anybody.

5 **A** I don't have enough money to pay for my ticket.
   B It's OK. I*'m going to lend* / *'ll lend* you some.

6 **A** You two look really shocked. What's the matter?
   B We just found out that we*'ll have* / *'re having* twins!

7 **A** I thought you'd just bought a new dishwasher.
   B We did. It*'s being* / *will be delivered* tomorrow.

8 **A** Can you meet me after work?
   B I'd love to, but John*'s taking* / *'ll take* me out for dinner tonight.

may / might / could for possibility

9 *We may go to Thailand*

Complete the sentences using the prompts.

1 We haven't decided what we're doing this summer.
   (may – go to Thailand / Hawaii)
   We may go to Thailand, or we may go to Hawaii.

2 Let's go and see that new movie.
   (could – be good / be terrible)
   _____

3 Kate doesn't know what she wants to do when she grows up.
   (might – be a doctor / vet)
   _____

4 I can't decide which car I want.
   (may – buy a Ford / Toyota)
   _____

5 There are two things I'd like to see on TV tonight.
   (could – watch a movie / the game)
   _____

All future forms

10 The lottery winners

1 Complete the text about the lottery winners using the future verb forms a–m.

a is buying	**d** might also upgrade	**g** is donating	**j** are putting	**l** 're going to give
b are going to spend	**e** won't change	**h** will help	**k** isn't leaving	**m** will continue
c 'll live	**f** may use	**i** may move in		

Lottery Winners just "Ordinary People"

What would you do if you won the lottery?
Would it change your life?

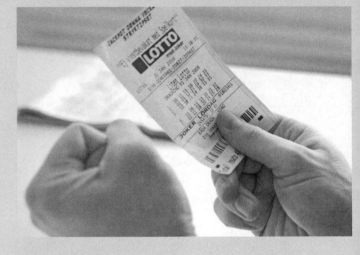

Joe and Rhonda Meath, winners of $11.7 million in the Minnesota Lottery, insist that it (1) ___ theirs. They're just ordinary people, they say, and they (2) ___ their lives as they always have.

Rhonda, 51, is a waitress, and she (3) ___ her job. She loves working at the Lake Elmo Inn, and her customers and coworkers love her, too. Joe, 53, has been retired for a few years since he injured his back, but he still helps his community by plowing snow in the winter.

Instead of changing their own lives, it seems like the Meaths (4) ___ the people around them. They (5) ___ money aside for their children and grandchildren, and Joe (6) ___ a house for his mother. Rhonda (7) ___ money to the St. Paul Police Canine Foundation, a local organization that trains police dogs, where she (8) ___ to volunteer. In addition, they (9) ___ $15,000 to the girl who sold them the winning ticket when she graduates high school to help her with college expenses.

Of course, the Meaths (10) ___ some of the money on themselves. They (11) ___ some of it to support their hobbies (Joe enjoys hunting, and Rhonda raises and shows German shepherds at dog shows). They (12) ___ their cars: Rhonda would like a new van to transport her dogs, and Joe is thinking about getting an RV.* However, instead of buying a huge new mansion to live in, the Meaths (13) ___ to a smaller home.

In the meantime, the new millionaires are just trying to get on with their usual routines. They're just ordinary people, after all!

*a large vehicle with kitchen, bathroom, and beds inside for traveling and camping

2 Here are the answers to some questions about the Meaths. Write the questions.

1 <u>How will winning the lottery change their lives</u> ? They say it won't change their lives.

2 _____ ? Because she loves her job.

3 _____ ? For their children and grandchildren.

4 _____ ? A new house.

5 _____ ? When she graduates high school.

6 _____ ? An RV.

Prepositions

11 Adjective + preposition

1 Complete these sentences using *of* or *with*.

1 You must be fed up _____ listening to me complaining about my work – how has your day been?

2 I've always been jealous _____ people who can sing well. Even my cat leaves the room when I start singing.

3 I've put a lot of work into this essay, and I'm really proud _____ it.

4 I thought I was getting a toothache, but the dentist said there's nothing wrong _____ my teeth at all.

2 Complete these sentences using *about* or *for*.

1 I feel really sorry _____ Lucy. First day of her vacation and she has the flu.

2 Are you serious _____ starting your own business? It's a very risky thing to do, you know.

3 We're very excited _____ going to Egypt. We've always wanted to see the pyramids.

4 I think it was Van Gogh who was famous _____ painting sunflowers, wasn't it?

3 Complete these sentences using *in* or *to*.

1 Are you and Jim interested _____ tennis? I think I can get some tickets for the U.S. Open next week.

2 You don't look at all similar _____ Mark. It's difficult to believe he's your brother.

3 Who's that woman over there dressed _____ black? I want someone to introduce me to her.

4 Thank you so much. I'll never forget how kind you've been _____ me.

4 Complete these sentences with the correct preposition.

1 **A** Did you try that new Italian restaurant?

   B Yeah. The food was OK, but I wasn't satisfied _____ the service.

2 It's typical _____ Bob to disappear when it's time to do the dishes!

3 **A** Excuse me, could you tell me where the post office is?

   B I'm sorry, I'm not familiar _____ this area myself.

4 **A** Good morning. *Grantech Solutions*.

   B Hello. I'd like to speak to the person responsible _____ recruitment, please.

Listening

12 Friends of the earth

1 🎧 Listen to three students, Debbie, Jake, and Steve, discussing whether to go to a protest at the local airport. Are these sentences true (✓) or false (✗)? Correct the false ones.

1 The airport already has two runways.
2 Air travel accounts for 15% of carbon dioxide emissions.
3 There is twice as much air travel as there was 15 years ago.
4 The protest will produce its own energy needs.
5 They decide to go to the protest on Tuesday.

2 Complete the lines from the conversation with the correct future form.

1 He _____ (meet) his counselor this afternoon to talk about changing majors.

2 Well, to be honest, I'm not so sure a protest _____ (make) a difference on this one.

3 … you think they _____ (ban) air travel some day soon, do you?

4 I _____ (not get) involved in anything illegal or violent.

5 I don't know if it's legal or illegal, but I'm sure it _____ (be) completely non-violent.

6 I _____ (pick) you both up at 10:00.

🎧 Listen again and check.

6 What matters to me

Information questions • Adjectives and adverbs • Antonyms
• Phrasal verbs in context • Word stress

Question forms

1 Matching questions and answers

1 Read the questionnaire. Write questions a–l in the correct place.

a How long have you been painting and sculpting?

b What are you inspired by?

c Which artist has influenced you the most?

d Whose genes did you inherit?

e Who do you live with?

f What's your apartment like?

g What's it like living in Miami?

h How much time do you spend in your studio every day?

i How often do you have exhibits?

j How many pieces have you sold?

k Who generally buys your work?

l What plans do you have for the future?

2 Find a question in exercise 1 with:

☐ *how* + adverb

☐ *what* + noun

☐ *which* + noun

☐ *whose* + noun

☐ *how much*

☐ *how many*

☐ a preposition at the end

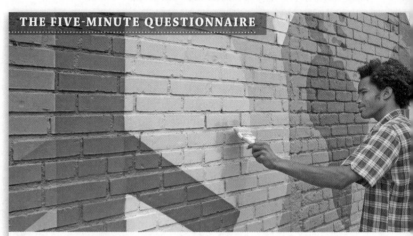

THE FIVE-MINUTE QUESTIONNAIRE

We chat with up-and-coming artist Simón Gutiérrez Loza about his life and his work.

1 _____ My cousin and his best friend.

2 _____ Hmm. That's a tough question. Probably Picasso.

3 _____ I'm always showing my work somewhere – in coffee shops, galleries, or outdoors on the walls in Wynwood, the art district.

4 _____ All types of people. I try not to price my work too high. I want it to be accessible.

5 _____ It's amazing! It's very international, and there's a huge art scene here. Also, I love the weather.

6 _____ I want to travel around the world; find new inspiration and maybe learn some new techniques.

7 _____ I'm definitely more like my mother. She's very laid back and creative. My father was much more serious and organized.

8 _____ Since I was two years old! I've always loved creating.

9 _____ I'm not sure, but more than 300.

10 _____ Anywhere from 15 minutes to 16 hours! It depends on my mood and what I'm working on.

11 _____ It's modern, and very cool. Of course, there are paintings and sculptures in every room.

12 _____ Nature… but also the human condition. Some of my work is political.

Questions

2 Questions with *what / which / whose*

Write a question with *what / which / whose* + noun.

1 Do you want to get up at 6:00? 7:00? 8:00?
   What time do you want to get up?

2 Are you looking for a small shirt? Medium? Large?

   _____

3 Is this Jane's coat? Annie's? Henry's?

   _____

4 Is your wife Brazilian? Spanish? Lebanese?

   _____

5 Do you read *The Times*? *The Post*? *USA Today*?

   _____

6 Do you like classical music? Rock 'n' roll? Jazz?

   _____

7 Did you go to Oxford University? The Sorbonne? Harvard?

   _____

8 Is your phone an LG? A Samsung? A Motorola?

   _____

9 Is it the 39 bus that goes to the station? The 18? Or the 103?

   _____

10 Is this my dictionary or your dictionary?

   _____

11 Is your house number 3? Number 33?

   _____

12 Do you want this one or that one?

   _____

3 Questions with *how*

Write a question with *how* + adjective / adverb.

1 " **How long** is the Panama Canal?"
   "About fifty miles from the Atlantic to the Pacific."

2 "_____ is it from your house to school?'
   "About three miles."

3 "_____ does it take you to get to school?'
   "Forty-five minutes if the traffic is OK."

4 "_____ can your car go?"
   "The top speed is 150 mph."

5 "_____ time do you spend watching TV?"
   "I guess about four hours a day."

6 "_____ times have you been on a plane?"
   "Three."

7 "_____ do you go to the dentist?"
   "Three or four times a year."

8 "_____ have you known your girlfriend?"
   "We were in school together, so all my life."

9 "_____ are you?"
   "I'm 6 feet tall."

10 "_____ did your baby weigh when she was born?"
   "7 pounds 5 ounces."

4 More questions

Match a question in **A** with an answer in **B**.

A
1 [b] What does this button do?
2 [ ] What is this remote control for?
3 [ ] What are your parents like?
4 [ ] How are your parents?
5 [ ] What are tennis rackets made of these days?
6 [ ] You shouted at him? What did you do that for?
7 [ ] How many of you are there?
8 [ ] What did you do to your leg?

B
a Graphite and titanium.
b It sets the timer.
c If you count the kids, there are ten of us.
d They're fine, thanks.
e I twisted my ankle playing basketball.
f Because he was really annoying me!
g It controls the stereo system.
h They're a lot of fun. Not too embarrassing.

5 Questions with a preposition

Complete the questions with a preposition at the end.

1 **A** I think Jamie's in love.
   B Who _is he_ in love _with_?
   A Beth, of course. He's crazy about her.

2 **A** Dad, can I have the car tonight?
   B What _____ want it _____?
   A I'm going out with a couple of friends. Is that OK?

3 **A** There's someone's phone on the table.
   Who _____ belong _____?
   B It's mine. Thanks.

4 **A** Jack's granddad died last week.
   B Oh, no! What _____ die _____?
   A A heart attack.

5 **A** I am REALLY angry.
   B What _____ so angry _____?
   A My bank has charged me $20 for being 50 cents overdrawn.

6 **A** Pierre's the CEO of a European company.
   B Really? Who _____ work _____?
   A *Allgemeine Union.*

7 **A** We can't go yet! Not everyone's here.
   B Who _____ waiting _____?
   A Anna. She's getting ready.

8 **A** Do you like my new dress?
   B Where _____ get it _____?
   A Beebo's at the mall.

9 **A** Mary got married last weekend.
   B Really! Who _____ get married _____?
   A A guy she met in Japan.

10 **A** I had a great conversation with Joe the other day.
   B Oh, yes? What _____ talk _____?
   A His relationship with his boss. Very interesting.

6 Questions in context

Look at Kathy's profile on her website.
Write the questions.

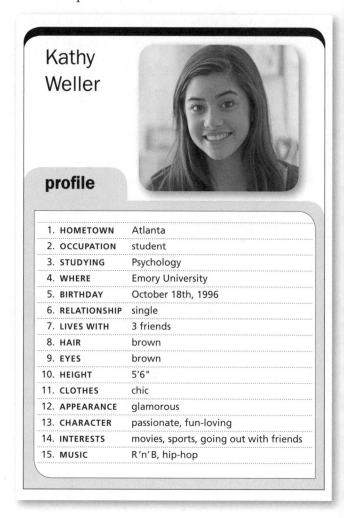

Kathy Weller

profile

1.	HOMETOWN	Atlanta
2.	OCCUPATION	student
3.	STUDYING	Psychology
4.	WHERE	Emory University
5.	BIRTHDAY	October 18th, 1996
6.	RELATIONSHIP	single
7.	LIVES WITH	3 friends
8.	HAIR	brown
9.	EYES	brown
10.	HEIGHT	5'6"
11.	CLOTHES	chic
12.	APPEARANCE	glamorous
13.	CHARACTER	passionate, fun-loving
14.	INTERESTS	movies, sports, going out with friends
15.	MUSIC	R'n'B, hip-hop

1 Where _does she live_ ?
2 What _does she do_ ?
3 _____ ?
4 Which _____ at?
5 _____ ?
6 _____ going out with anyone?
7 _____ ?
8 _____ ?
9 _____ ?
10 How _____ ?
11 What sort _____ ?
12 _____ look like?
13 _____ like as a person?
14 _____ like doing?
15 What kind _____ ?

Tenses and questions

7 A place of my own

1 Read about Sicily's tiny house. Put the verb forms from the box in the correct place in the text.

didn't want	began	was given
's looking forward	had been killed	was making
~~build~~	taught	was researching

Middle Schooler Builds Her Own Small House

While most 12-year olds (1) _____**build**_____ little toy houses out of Lego, Sicily Kolbeck of Marietta, Georgia (2) _____ a much more ambitious project: designing and building a real "tiny house" out of wood – and no, not tiny as in doll-sized. Tiny houses are small homes that measure between 100–400 square feet. People actually live in them!

Sicily came upon the idea to build a tiny house while she (3) _____ ideas for a school project. To get started, she (4) _____ a large amount of money by her mother and she also launched a fundraising campaign online. She also started a blog, *La Petite Maison*, to track her project. Her father, a sailor and woodworker, (5) _____ her about construction basics, such as how to cut wood and how to use power tools. Soon, Sicily (6) _____ excellent progress with the help of her parents.

Then, tragedy struck. Mrs. Kolbeck received a call in the middle of the night with news that her husband (7) _____ in a car accident. Sicily was heartbroken. For a time, she (8) _____ to do much at all. But

during a road trip with her mother, she realized that she had to finish what she had started. She wanted to do it for her father.

Sicily was able to finish building her 128 square foot cozy blue house by the time she turned 14, and for less than $10,000. It includes a little kitchen and bathroom, a small reading area, a loft sleeping area, and some art on the walls, including a photo of her father's boat. She (9) _____ to more projects in the future. She stays in the little house sometimes, but someday maybe she'll move in full-time!

2 Complete the questions.

1 How long _did it take Sicily to build the house_____? Around two years.

2 _____ like inside? It's very small, but cozy, with art on the walls.

3 _____ on her wall? A picture of her father's boat.

4 _____ ? She was 12 years old.

5 _____ ? 128 square feet.

6 _____ ? Under $10,000.

7 _____ inspired by? Her father.

8 _____ ? Maybe someday.

Adjectives

8 -ed/-ing adjectives

1 Complete the story about Happy Hannah. Use the words in parentheses. Add -ed or -ing. Sometimes the spelling changes.

Happy Hannah

Happy Hannah thinks her job is
(1) **exciting** (excite) because it's very
varied. It isn't easy, and she has to
work hard, but she likes it, so it's
(2) _____ (reward) as well.

If her clients are (3) _____ (satisfy) with the service they
get from her, Hannah is happy. When she meets her targets, and her boss
tells her she's wonderful, she's (4) _____ (delight), obviously.

Hannah has an apartment with (5) _____ (stun) views over the
city. Her boyfriend, Freddy, who has a (6) _____ (challenge) job in
the city, is (7) _____ (overwhelm) by her beauty and totally
in love with her. She is (8) _____ (amuse) by him because he
tells such funny stories.

2 Complete the story about Depressed Dave. Use the words from
the box below. Add -ed or -ing. Sometimes the spelling changes.

| confuse | terrify | worry | annoy | ~~disappoint~~ | exhaust | impress |

Depressed Dave

Depressed Dave is (1) **disappointed**
because he didn't get a pay raise.
He's in a lot of debt, so he's very
(2) _____ about money at
the moment.

On top of all that, he isn't sleeping
well, so he always arrives at work feeling
(3) _____ . As he's new at the job,
there's a lot he doesn't understand. People tell him different information, he
doesn't know what to do, which is very (4) _____ for him.
And to make matters worse, his boss is a bit of a bully, so poor Dave is
(5) _____ of her. She doesn't like Dave, the way he talks, and she
isn't (6) _____ by the way he dresses, either. In fact, she is pretty
(7) _____ by everything about him.

Adverbs

9 Position of adverbs

Adverbs sound better in a certain position.
I often get headaches.
I like modern art very much.

Put the adverbs in the correct place in the
sentence.

1 You'll succeed if you don't work hard.
(never)

_____

2 I've finished my homework but not quite.
(almost)

_____

3 She's coming to the party. (definitely)

_____

4 You behaved yesterday. I'm ashamed of you.
(very badly)

_____

5 They love each other. (deeply)

_____

6 I don't like her. (really)

_____

7 He earns $20,000 a year. (only)

_____

8 He always wears a sweater, in the summer.
(even)

_____

9 The water isn't warm to go swimming.
(enough)

_____

10 It's cold for me. (too / much)

_____

11 I want a cup of coffee. (just)

_____

12 He wasn't injured. (fortunately, / seriously)

_____

13 I forgot her birthday. (completely)

_____

14 I don't like skiing. (at all / very much)

_____

15 When did you see Peter? (last)

_____

Vocabulary

10 Antonyms

1 Match an adjective in **A** with its opposite in **B**.

A		B	
1 ☐	hardworking	a	part-time
2 ☐	old-fashioned	b	stressful
3 ☐	casual	c	lazy
4 ☐	good-looking	d	sharp
5 ☐	full-time	e	rude
6 ☐	polite	f	modern
7 ☐	relaxing	g	unattractive

A		B	
1 ☐	easygoing	a	stupid
2 ☐	poor	b	cruel
3 ☐	bad-tempered	c	calm
4 ☐	second-hand	d	fussy
5 ☐	smart	e	modest
6 ☐	kind	f	well off
7 ☐	big-headed	g	brand new

2 Complete the sentences with a word from the boxes in exercise 1.

1 **A** "He isn't very polite, is he?"
  B "No. In fact, he's incredibly _rude_ ."

2 **A** "They need to modernize the way they work."
  B "True. Some of their business practices are very _____."

3 **A** "Camping is not a relaxing vacation, is it?"
  B "That's true. It's a very _____ way of spending a vacation."

4 **A** "Jane's such a lazy person."
  B "Strange. Her brother is very _____."

5 You can't wear jeans to an interview! You have to look _____!

6 My girlfriend gets angry about everything. She's so _____.

7 George's kids are such _____ eaters. They don't eat bread, or cheese, or anything green. They only eat pasta.

8 **A** "I'm so stupid. I ran out of gas on the highway."
  B "Yeah, that wasn't very _____."

9 Pete's always talking about how much money he has, the fabulous vacations he takes, and how intelligent he is. He's so _____.

10 I know Pete has money, but really he isn't that _____. He owes the bank a lot.

Pronunciation

11 Word stress

1 The unstressed syllables in words are often pronounced as the weak sound /ə/.

This is the most common vowel sound in spoken English.

/ə/	/ə/ /ə/	/ə/ /ə/
global	policeman	performance

🎧 Listen and repeat.

2 🎧 Listen to these words. Write in the /ə/ sounds.

/ə/ /ə/ conversation	politeness	banana
attention	sociable	preparation
apartment	international	customer
personal	intelligent	surprising

🎧 Listen again and repeat.

3 Complete the sentences with another form of the word in **bold**. Mark the /ə/ sound in both words.

1 I love his **photographs**. He's definitely my
   favorite _photographer_ .

2 Dave studied **politics** in college, but he never wanted to become a _____.

3 **Technology** advances so quickly these days. It's impossible to imagine what _____ changes there will be in the next 20 years.

4 Bill doesn't seem to like **vegetables**. I can't understand why he's a _____.

5 The role of **employment** agencies is to help _____ find suitable workers.

6 I know anything's **possible** in soccer, but do you think the U.S. ever winning the World Cup is a real _____?

🎧 Listen and check. Repeat the sentences, paying attention to the /ə/ sounds in both words.

Phrasal verbs

12 Phrasal verbs in context (1)

Complete the conversations with a phrasal verb from the box in the correct form. The definitions in parentheses will help you.

Trips			
get going	pick up	hold on	get in

A You're arriving in New York next Monday, right?
B Yes, that's right.
A I'll (1) _____ you _____ (come and get) if you like.
B That would be great.
A What time does your train (2) _____ (arrive)?
B (3) _____ (Wait), I'll just check on the ticket. Um…5:45.
A OK. The traffic's bad at that time, but if I (4) _____
   (leave the house) at about 5:00 P.M., I'll be there in plenty of time.

Relationships			
put up with	split up	get over	go out (with someone)

A Did you hear that Sam and Dee have (9) _____
   (end a relationship, separate)?
B Really? They've been (10) _____ (be boyfriend and
   girlfriend) for years! What went wrong?
A Sam said all they did was argue, and he couldn't (11) _____
   (tolerate) it anymore. Dee apparently is very upset.
B I'm sure she is, but she'll (12) _____ (begin to feel better) it.
   He wasn't that great.

Moving			
get down to	bring up	work out	settle in

A I hear you just moved. How (5) _____ you _____ (adapt to your
   new surroundings)?
B Not bad. It's all a little chaotic, so it's hard to (6) _____
   (finally start doing) work.
A And the kids?
B Well, we moved to the country because we didn't want to
   (7) _____ them _____ (educate and care for) in the city. They're
   finding it tough right now. They left their friends behind.
A I'm sure it will all (8) _____ (get better). Give it time.

Hurry up!			
hold up	go on about	calm down	come on

A (13) _____ (hurry up)! We're late!
B All right! There's no need to panic. (14) _____ (become less
   agitated)!
A Get moving! How long does it take you to get ready?
B There's no need to (15) _____ (talk endlessly in an annoying
   way) it. I'm moving as fast as I can.
A But we might get (16) _____ (make late) in traffic.
   Then we'd be really late.

Listening

13 My favorite room

1 🎧 Listen to Dan and Laura talking about their
favorite room in their homes. Complete the chart.

	Dan	Laura
Room	attic room	
Size		pretty big
Flooring	wooden, floorboards	
Wall color		a warm shade of blue
Furniture	coffee table, sofa, lamp	
Windows		huge bay window

2 Choose the correct answer.

1 It feels so *good* / *well* to have more space.
2 … especially when the kids are being *noisy* / *noisily*.
3 That sounds *wonderful* / *wonderfully* old-fashioned!
4 … when I want to read, or even to just sit
   quiet / *quietly* on my own for a while.
5 … blues can be quite cold if you don't choose
   careful / *carefully*.
6 … if you can't find anything you like in the stores,
   you have to get *creative* / *creatively*, don't you?
7 … even in winter, especially in the morning when
   the sun shines *straight* / *straightly* into it.
8 I like to wake up *slow* / *slowly* as I watch the first
   people setting off for work.

🎧 Listen again and check.

7 Fashions and passions

Present Perfect Simple and Continuous – active and passive
• Prepositions – noun + preposition • *be* and *have* • sentence stress

Present Perfect or Simple Past?

1 Who's who?

1 Match the sentences with the people.

1 [b] He's lived in New York since 2010. His blog *Humans of New York* has been very successful.

2 [ ] She married three times. She died when she was 36.

3 [ ] She has won several awards for both her acting and singing careers.

4 [ ] She's been with the American Ballet Theater since 2000, but she's danced ballet since she was 13.

5 [ ] She's written seven Harry Potter books. She's been writing stories since 1971.

6 [ ] She wrote *Pride and Prejudice* when she was in her twenties.

7 [ ] He was one of the most influential filmmakers of his time. He directed 30 films during his career.

8 [ ] His band was called *The Wailers*. He died of a brain tumor at the age of 36.

2 Complete the questions about the people using the Present Perfect or the Simple Past.

3 Write the answers to the questions in the boxes a–h.

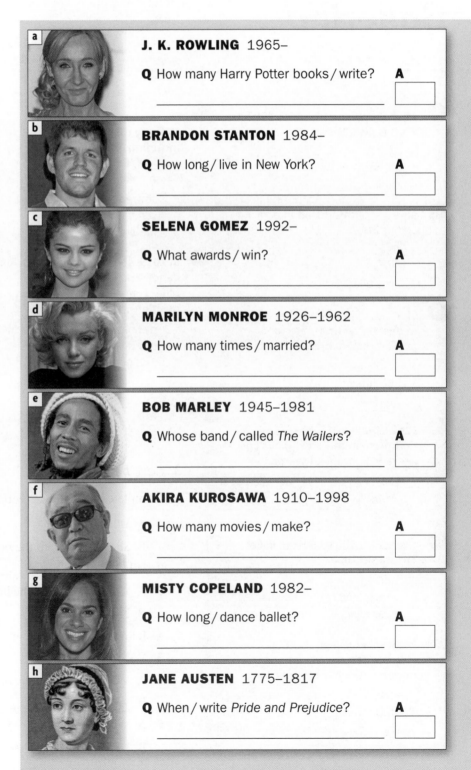

a **J. K. ROWLING** 1965–
Q How many Harry Potter books / write? **A** [ ]

b **BRANDON STANTON** 1984–
Q How long / live in New York? **A** [ ]

c **SELENA GOMEZ** 1992–
Q What awards / win? **A** [ ]

d **MARILYN MONROE** 1926–1962
Q How many times / married? **A** [ ]

e **BOB MARLEY** 1945–1981
Q Whose band / called *The Wailers*? **A** [ ]

f **AKIRA KUROSAWA** 1910–1998
Q How many movies / make? **A** [ ]

g **MISTY COPELAND** 1982–
Q How long / dance ballet? **A** [ ]

h **JANE AUSTEN** 1775–1817
Q When / write *Pride and Prejudice*? **A** [ ]

2 Choosing the correct tense

Read more about the life of Misty Copeland.
Put a check (✓) next to the correct form of the verb.

An Unlikely Ballerina

1 Misty Copeland _____ in 1982 in Kansas City, Missouri.
- ○ born
- ○ is born
- ○ was born

2 She _____ interested in dancing all her life.
- ○ is
- ○ was
- ○ has been

3 She _____ her first ballet class at age 13, which is late for a professional dancer.
- ○ took
- ○ has taken
- ○ was taken

4 When she was 15, she _____ first place in the prestigious Los Angeles Spotlight Awards.
- ○ has won
- ○ wins
- ○ won

5 She _____ the American Ballet Theater in 2000.
- ○ joined
- ○ has joined
- ○ was joined

6 Early in her career, she _____ criticism because of her unconventionally curvy body.
- ○ faced
- ○ has faced
- ○ has been faced

7 During her career, she _____ in many major productions, including *The Nutcracker*, *Firebird*, *Coppelia*, and *Swan Lake*.
- ○ starred
- ○ stars
- ○ has starred

8 In 2015, she _____ as a principal dancer for the ABT, the first black female to achieve that position.
- ○ has named
- ○ has been named
- ○ was named

9 In addition to dancing, Copeland _____ a memoir entitled *Life In Motion: An Unlikely Ballerina.*
- ○ has recently published
- ○ has recently been published
- ○ was recently published

10 Currently, New Line Cinema _____ a film based on Copeland's life.
- ○ is producing
- ○ produces
- ○ has produced

3 *have been* or *went*?

Complete the sentences with *have been* or *went*.

1 **A** Where's Mom?

   B She _____ to the post office.

2 Where _____ you _____ ? You're home so late!

3 **A** Are you going to the library today?

   B No, I already _____ yesterday.

4 If anyone calls, tell them I _____ to lunch. I'll be back at two.

5 We _____ never _____ to Japan, but we'd like to go.

6 **A** When are you going on vacation?

   B We already _____ . We _____ to Florida.

7 **A** What happened to your neighbors?

   B Didn't I tell you? They _____ to live in the south of France.

4 Time expressions

1 Put the word in parentheses in the correct place in the sentences.

1 I heard about your accident. (just)
2 Have you had breakfast? (yet)
3 I finished my exams. (already)
4 Have you been to Thailand? (ever)
5 I haven't seen that movie. (yet)

2 Rewrite the sentences using *for, since,* and *ago.*

1 I last saw him in 2010.

a (for) _____

b (since) _____

c (ago) _____

2 She went to Korea in April.

a (for) _____

b (since) _____

c (ago) _____

3 Read the situations below. What would you say? Use a time expression from exercises 1 and 2.

1 You're having lunch in a cafe. You stop eating for a minute and the waiter tries to take your plate away.

Excuse me! _____. (not finish)

2 You had a cup of coffee. Your sister comes in and offers you another cup.

No, thanks. _____ (have) one.

3 Tom went out two minutes ago. The phone rings. It's someone for Tom.

_____. (go out)

4 You rush home to see the World Cup final on TV. You want to know if you've missed the beginning.

_____? (start)

5 It's 9 P.M. You're watching TV. You finished your homework at 8 P.M. Your mom asks why you're not doing your homework.

But _____. (finish)

6 You meet an old friend. You can't remember when you last met.

How long _____? (meet)

Present Perfect passive

5 Active or passive?

Choose the correct verb form.

1 Angela *'s just promoted / 's just been promoted* to area manager of Latin America.

2 I *'ve applied / 've been applied* for a job.

3 How many times *have you injured / have you been injured* playing football?

4 Bob's wife *has just lost / has just been lost* her job.

5 My sister *has passed / has been passed* her final exams.

6 My brother *has given / has been given* tickets to the concert.

7 How much money *have you saved / have you been saved* for your around-the-world trip?

8 A strike *has called / has been called* by the air traffic controllers.

9 They *haven't offered / haven't been offered* more money by the management.

10 The population of our city *has risen / has been risen* to nearly a million.

Present Perfect Continuous

6 Simple or Continuous?

Choose the correct form of the verb.

1 I don't believe it! Somebody has *eaten* / *been eating* my chocolates! They're nearly all gone!
2 How many cookies have you *eaten* / *been eating* today?
3 I have never *met* / *been meeting* a nicer person in my life.
4 How long have you *known* / *been knowing* Charles and Lisa?
5 He's *written* / *been writing* a book for nearly a year. It'll be finished soon.
6 He's *written* / *been writing* a book. I saw it in the bookstore.
7 The children are very quiet. They've *watched* / *been watching* videos all morning.
8 They've *watched* / *been watching* five already.

7 Producing Simple or Continuous

Complete the sentences with the correct form of the verb in parentheses, Present Perfect Simple or Continuous.

1 Someone _____ (move) my car keys.
   I _____ (look) for them for hours, but
   I _____ (not find) them yet.
2 I _____ (shop) all morning,
   but I _____ (not buy) anything.
3 That's one of the best jokes I _____ ever
   _____ . (hear)
4 I _____ (listen) to
   you for the past half an hour, but I'm afraid I
   _____ (not understand) a single word.
5 A Are you all right? You look terrible!
   B No, I _____ (work) on the
      computer for hours, and I have a headache.
6 I _____ (try) to lose weight for
   months.
   I _____ (lose) five pounds so far.

8 Replying with questions

Complete the questions with either the Present Perfect Simple or Continuous.

1 A Esteban is a singer in a band.
   B *How long has he been singing in the band?*
      How many records has he made?
2 A I'm taking driving lessons.
   B How long _____ ?
      How many _____ ?
3 A Jiri is a teacher.
   B How long _____ ?
      How many schools _____ ?
4 A At last! You said you'd be here hours ago.
   B I'm sorry. How long _____ ?
5 A Anna is getting married to Ian next week.
   B How many _____ to the
      wedding?
      How long _____ Ian?
6 A What a surprise! I haven't seen you for years.
      What _____ all this time?
   B I've been abroad, actually.
   A Where _____ been?

9 Correcting mistakes

Correct the mistakes in these sentences.

1 How long do you know the teacher?
   _____

2 This is the first time I eat Thai food.
   _____

3 I learn English for four years now.
   _____

4 What have you done last night at around 8 P.M.?
   _____

5 How long you been working here?
   _____

6 The World Cup has won by Brazil five times.
   _____

Tense review

10 America's next extreme sport

1 Complete the article with the correct form of the verbs in parentheses. Use Present Perfect Simple or Continuous, and the Simple Past, active or passive.

Back to the Middle Ages

Jousting, a fighting sport that (1) _____ (become) popular in Europe during the Middle Ages, (2) _____ (make) somewhat of a comeback in the last couple of decades. A joust involves two knights in heavy armor who ride on horseback towards each other holding long lances. Each knight tries to knock the other off the horse.

Jousts first (3) _____ (reappear) in the 1970s, both in Europe and at American Renaissance fairs. Renaissance fairs (4) _____ (begin) in California in the 1960s and (5) _____ (become) very popular throughout the United States since then. At these events, actors dress in clothing styles from 500 years ago and give performances. Renaissance fair jousts (6) _____ (start) as theatrical productions with staged fights. The hits weren't real, and the moves and the winner (7) _____ (plan) before the show. However, since the 1970s and 80s, many groups (8) _____ (do) real full-contact jousts.

One such group is the Free Lancers, led by Roy Cox and his wife Kate, who (9) _____ (perform) jousts since 1989. They live like real knights used to live during medieval times. They travel around the country, sleep in tents, take care of the horses, and fight in shows and competitions.

Jousting is hard work – and it can be dangerous. Kate Cox (10) _____ often _____ (injure). She (11) _____ (break) her hand several times, and she (12) _____ (dislocate) her shoulder, too. The knights often get bumps and bruises when they fall from their horses. However, there (13) _____ (be) even more serious injuries. For example, one jouster (14) _____ (kill) in England in 2011 when a lance went through his helmet and into his eye – the same injury that (15) _____ (kill) King Henry II of France during a jousting tournament in 1559!

2 Here are some answers to questions about competitive jousting. Write the questions.

1 <u>How long have performers been fighting in real full-contact jousts?</u>
Since the 1970s and 80s.

2 _____ ?
In Europe during the Middle Ages.

3 _____ ?
In California.

4 _____ ?
Since 1989.

5 _____ ?
They first were theatrical productions with staged fights.

6 _____ ?
Yes, she has. She's broken her hand several times and dislocated her shoulder.

7 _____ ?
A lance went through his helmet and into his eye.

8 _____ ?
In 1559.

Vocabulary

11 *be* and *have*

1 There are many expressions formed with the verbs *be* and *have*. Match *be* and *have* with their expressions

crazy about	about to	a lot in common	fun
a problem (with)	sure of	time off work	into
off (work)	a word with	interested in	
in touch (with)	away on business	a great time	

be	have

2 Read conversations 1–3 and complete them with the correct form of the expressions from exercise 1.

1 **A** Do you like Jen?
   B Like her! I'm _____ her.
   A I didn't think she was your type.
   B What do you mean? We _____ a great time together. We have a lot _____ .
   A Really?
   B Well, yes. She likes opera and so do I.
   A What? Since when have you been _____ opera?
   B Well, I am now.

2 **A** Can I have _____ with you?
   B What about?
   A Well, you've had a lot of time _____ work lately.
   B I'm sorry.
   A You _____ off four times last month.
   B I know, I've _____ a lot of family problems.
   A What kind of problems?
   B Um—I'd rather not say.

3 **A** I'll miss you.
   B I'll miss you too.
   A You're _____ on business so much.
   B Don't worry. I'll be in _____ as soon as I get there.
   A Look, you have to go. Your flight's _____ to board.
   B Bye. Don't _____ too much fun while I'm away.
   A You can be _____ of that! Bye, _____ a good time!

Prepositions

12 Noun + preposition

Complete the sentences with a preposition from the box.

| on (x 3) | to (x 3) | in (x 3) |
| with | by | between |

1 What's the difference _____ *lend* and *borrow*?
2 There's been a big change _____ the weather recently.
3 We need to find a solution _____ this problem.
4 How much do you spend on food every week _____ average?
5 The trouble _____ you is that you don't listen to anybody.
6 I can't get access _____ my Internet bank account at the moment.
7 Tim didn't break your camera _____ purpose. It was an accident!
8 Congratulations _____ your engagement! When's the wedding?
9 Be careful what you say to Adam, he's _____ a bad mood today.
10 There's been a huge increase _____ gun crime recently.
11 I don't think there's really an alternative _____ traveling by air sometimes.
12 There are no rules for prepositions, you just have to learn them _____ heart.

Pronunciation

13 Sentence stress

1 The main stress in a sentence is on the words that give key (important) information.

🎧 Listen to the beginning of a conversation in a menswear department.

A	Can I <u>help</u> you?
C	<u>Yes</u>, please. I'm looking for a <u>sweater</u>.
A	What <u>size</u> are you?

🎧 We understand the message with just the key words.

A	Help?
C	Yes. Sweater.
A	Size?

2 Read the conversation and <u>underline</u> the words that give key information. (The number in parentheses shows how many words to underline in each line.)

A	Can I help you?	(1)
C	Yes, please. I'm looking for a sweater.	(2)
A	What size are you?	(1)
C	I usually wear a large.	(1)
A	And what color are you looking for?	(1)
C	Some kind of green.	(1)
A	What about this one? Do you like this?	(2)
C	No, I think the style is nice, but it's too bright.	(5)
A	Well what about this one then? It's a much darker green.	(3)
C	Oh, yes, I like that one much better. Is it made of cotton?	(4)
A	Yes, and it's machine-washable.	(3)
C	That's great. Can I try it on?	(3)
A	Of course. The dressing rooms are over there.	(5)

3 🎧 Listen to the conversation. Notice the stress on the key words. Listen and repeat.

Listening

14 Applying for a film degree

1 🎧 Listen to Jenny talking to one of the teachers at the Empire Film School about courses in film-making. Complete the advertisement.

EMPIRE Film School

Are you interested in a Degree in Film-making?

The Empire Film School has places available for students who

> have a real (1) _____ for film.
> (2) _____ their own films for some time.
> (3) _____ of directing.

Our graduates have found work in

> *feature films*
> (4) _____
> *commercials*
> (5) _____

The degree includes a class on the use of (6) _____ in film.

There are also places available on our Foundation Program, which provides (7) _____ experience of scriptwriting, (8) _____, camera work, and direction.

Interviews held in (9) _____ and (10) _____.

Apply in writing to the Admissions Officer.

2 🎧 Listen again. Are the sentences true (✓) or false (✗)? Correct the false ones.

1 Jenny has been crazy about film since she did her Film Studies program.
2 The counselor thinks qualifications are not the only important things for getting jobs in the film industry.
3 Some recent graduates made a feature film that's won a prize.
4 Jenny used a lot of music in the films she made.
5 She isn't sure which area of film she wants to specialize in in the future.
6 The Foundation Program lasts two months, from May until June.

8 No fear!

Verb patterns • Phrasal verb without a noun • Weak sounds/sentence stress

Verb patterns

1 Going to work in Africa

1 Read the conversation between Alan and Betty.
<u>Underline</u> the correct verb pattern.

GOING TO WORK IN AFRICA

Alan I'm thinking of (1) *apply* / <u>*applying*</u> for a job in East Africa, in Tanzania.

Betty Really? I used (2) *living* / *to live* there.

A I know, I remember you (3) *saying* / *to say*. I'd like (4) *asking* / *to ask* you about it, if that's OK.

B Go ahead. I'll do my best (5) *remembering* / *to remember*. I was there for two years, but that was ten years ago.

A So, what was it like?

B It was a great experience. I liked everything except the climate. I didn't enjoy (6) *working* / *to work* in the heat.

A Ah, I can't help (7) *worrying* / *to worry* about the heat. Was it really difficult (8) *keep* / *to keep* cool?

B Not if you are lucky enough (9) *having* / *to have* air-conditioning, but we just had fans. And we were on the coast, near Dar es Salaam, and it's really hot and humid there. Where is your job based?

A A town called Arusha.

B Oh, very nice. That's much cooler, inland, near Mt. Kilimanjaro. I'll never forget (10) *climbing* / *to climb* Kilimanjaro.

A Oh, I'd love (11) *doing* / *to do* that and go on safari. Did you manage (12) *travel* / *to travel* around much?

B Oh yes, we went to most of the big game parks – you know, like the Serengeti Plain and the Ngorongoro Crater – that was so huge it made me (13) *feel* / *to feel* very small, and the wildlife was amazing. Once, on the Serengeti, a whole family of monkeys decided (14) *playing* / *to play* on the roof of our car. We didn't dare (15) *moving* / *move*.

A Which animals did you like best?

B Actually, I think it was the giraffes. I loved (16) *watching* / *watch* the way they raise their long necks to eat. Oh, and the lions, of course. Do you know that in Lake Manyara National Park the lions actually climb trees?

A Really? It all sounds so exciting. I'm definitely going to apply for the job. It's been great (17) *talk* / *talking* to you.

B Give me a call, and let me (18) *know* / *to know* if you go.

2 🎧 Listen and check.

3 Complete this summary of the conversation with the verb in parentheses in the correct form.

Alan is thinking of (1) __applying__ (apply) for a job in Tanzania. He asks Betty (2) _____ (tell) him about it because she used (3) _____ (live) there. She tries (4) _____ (remember) what it was like. She says she found it difficult (5) _____ (work) in the heat, and the problem with (6) _____ (live) on the coast was that it was very hot and humid. However, she really enjoyed (7) _____ (go) on safari and loved (8) _____ (visit) the game parks. She saw lions (9) _____ (sleep) in trees, and once lots of monkeys started (10) _____ (play) on the roof of her car. Betty helped Alan (11) _____ (make) up his mind about the job, and he's decided (12) _____ (apply) for it. He's promised (13) _____ (call) Betty and let her (14) _____ (know) if he gets it.

▶▶ **Verb Patterns p. 90**

2 *-ing* forms

Complete the sentences with the *-ing* form of the verbs in the box.

walk	give up	~~wonder~~	fix	work
help	wake up	find	watch	live

1 I can't help __wondering__ what life in Africa will be like.
2 _____ too much TV is bad for your eyes.
3 I'll repair your watch for you. I'm good at _____ things.
4 _____ a really good job these days is really difficult.
5 My children are afraid of _____ in the dark, so we keep a light on at night.
6 Did you know that _____ is one of the best forms of exercise?
7 Thank you for _____ me. I really appreciate it.
8 _____ in a big city can be very stressful.
9 _____ sweets is easy. I've done it hundreds of times!
10 I earned a lot of money by _____ overtime.

3 Infinitives with or without *to*

Complete the sentences with the infinitive form of the verbs in the box.

buy	~~pay~~	follow	join	stay
be	carry	learn	hurt	show

1 We can't afford __to pay__ all our monthly bills.
2 It's impossible _____ these instructions.
3 Let me _____ you how to do it.
4 I'm so sorry, I didn't mean _____ your feelings.
5 The teacher made the children _____ after school.
6 I want my children _____ to play a musical instrument.
7 My son persuaded me _____ the latest cell phone.
8 Can you help me _____ this box upstairs?
9 I've invited Mr. Smith _____ us after the meeting.
10 My parents have always encouraged me _____ independent.

4 Which two are possible?

Read the sentences. Which two verbs or phrases can fill the gap?

1 The teacher _____ me to be more careful with my work in the future.

   (a) told **(b)** would like **c** hopes

2 I _____ eating fast food when I was in college.

   a gave up **b** couldn't afford **c** started

3 She _____ to help me paint the kitchen.

   a enjoyed **b** promised **c** offered

4 I _____ going to Mexico next year.

   a am looking forward to **b** would love **c** am thinking of

5 My father _____ me to take driving lessons when I was seventeen.

   a let **b** wanted **c** allowed

6 I'm _____ to have a big party for my next birthday.

   a looking forward **b** planning **c** hoping

7 We _____ to find a parking space in the city center.

   a tried **b** didn't manage **c** succeeded

8 I _____ driving in the rush hour.

   a don't want **b** can't stand **c** loathe

5 Reporting verbs + infinitive

Complete the lines and rewrite the sentences to mean the same.

1 "Please can you translate this sentence for me?" Maria said to Mark.

   Maria asked **Mark to translate the sentence for her.**

2 "Please, please marry me. I can't live without you," Tom said to Mia.

   Tom begged _____

3 "Don't run around the edge of the swimming pool, or you'll fall in," Mary said to her children.

   Mary warned _____

4 "I won't go to bed!" Bobby said.

   Bobby refused _____

5 "You should talk to your lawyer," Ben said to Bill.

   Ben advised _____

6 "Take that chewing gum out of your mouth immediately!" the teacher said to Harry.

   The teacher ordered _____

6 Using a dictionary

Look at the extract from the *Oxford Wordpower Dictionary*. It shows all the possible verb patterns for the verb *agree*.

> **agree** /əˈgriː/ *verb*
> ➤ SHARE OPINION **1** [I] **agree (with sb/sth); agree (that…)** to have the same opinion as sb/sth: *"I think we should talk to the manager about this." "Yes, I agree."* ✦ *I agree with Paul.* ✦ *Do you agree that we should travel by train?* ✦ *I'm afraid I don't agree.* **OPP** disagree
> ➤ SAY YES **2** [I] **agree (to sth/to do sth)** to say yes to sth: *I asked my boss if I could go home early and she agreed.* ✦ *Alkis has agreed to lend me his car for the weekend.* **OPP** refuse
> ➤ ARRANGE **3** [I,T] **agree (to do sth); agree (on sth)** to make an arrangement or decide sth with sb: *They agreed to meet the following day.* ✦ *Can we agree on a price?* ✦ *We agreed a price of $500.*
> ➤ APPROVE OF **4** [I] **agree with sth** to think that sth is right: *I don't agree with experiments on animals.*
> ➤ BE THE SAME **5** [I] to be the same as sth: *The two accounts of the accident do not agree.*
> **IDM** **not agree with sb** (used about food) to make sb feel ill

Extract from Oxford Wordpower Dictionary, 3rd edition © Oxford University Press 2006

Read the sentences and check with the extract. Is the verb pattern correct (✔) or incorrect (✗)? Rewrite the incorrect ones.

1 Alan thinks it's too expensive, and I'm agree.

   _____

2 She thinks she's right, but I'm not agree.

   _____

3 I don't agree with you.

   _____

4 All doctors agree that not exercising is bad for your health.

   _____

5 She thought we should go, and I agreed it.

   _____

6 They agreed talking about it again tomorrow.

   _____

7 A dangerous moment

1 Read about Dennis Gibney's dangerous moment. Complete the text with the correct words in the boxes.

SAVED BY AN ELEPHANT!

| to accompany | ~~training~~ | to go | not very easy | let | to see |

After (1) **training** for five years to be a doctor, Dennis Gibney wanted (2) _____ more of the world, so he took a job in a hospital in Kathmandu, the capital city of Nepal. It was hard work, and after a couple of months the hospital (3) _____ him have a few days' vacation. He decided that he'd like (4) _____ into the jungle. This is (5) _____ to do on your own, so he asked a Nepalese guide, Adesh, (6) _____ him.

| was hoping | made | carrying | to protect | was about to | meeting |

They set off at 6 o'clock one morning, with two elephants (7) _____ their equipment. It was hot and humid, especially as Adesh had (8) _____ Dennis buy special thick shoes and trousers (9) _____ him from snakes. Dennis (10) _____ to see lots of wildlife, particularly tigers, because as a child he had always dreamed of (11) _____ a tiger. His childhood dream (12) _____ come true!

2 Complete the lines of conversation between Adesh and Dennis.

It was afternoon, and Adesh told Dennis not to expect to see any tigers because they usually like to sleep in the heat of the day. However, suddenly, in the distance they saw one. Adesh ordered Dennis to keep very quiet. They crept nearer and found a dying deer, lying in the bushes – the tiger's lunch. They could no longer see the tiger, but somehow they could feel his presence. Dennis didn't dare move or breathe. He looked up and found himself staring into a pair of large yellow eyes. The tiger roared and tried to grab his leg. Adesh managed to pull him away, but they had no real hope of escaping. Then, incredibly, one of the elephants appeared. It ran at the tiger, which turned and fled.

They say elephants never forget, but Dennis and Adesh will certainly never forget that it was an elephant that saved their lives.

a "Don't expect _____."

b "Tigers usually _____."

c "Ssshh! I told you _____."

d "What's that _____ in the bushes?"

e "I'm afraid to _____."

f "Help! The tiger's trying _____."

g "We have no hope of _____."

h "The elephant's managed to_____."

Phrasal verbs

8 Phrasal verb without a noun

1 Complete the groups of sentences with the correct form of a phrasal verb from the box.

a **up** can mean *more*

speak hurry save ~~fill~~	up

1 We're going on a long drive. I'll **fill up** with gas.

2 If we want to have a vacation this year, we'll have to _____ .

3 We're late! If you don't _____ , we'll miss the plane.

4 I can't hear you! Can you _____ ?

b **down** can mean *less*

calm slow go cut	down

1 I want to lose weight, so I've _____ the amount I eat.

2 You're driving too fast! Please _____ !

3 My temperature was 42°, now it's 39°, so it's _____ .

4 Stop getting so upset about things that don't matter. _____ !

c **out** can mean *end*

drop die go figure	out

1 I'm trying to _____ how much you owe me.

2 Tim _____ of school because he found it too difficult.

3 The fire _____ because we didn't put enough wood on.

4 Tigers are killed for their skins. They're _____ in the wild.

2 Complete the sentences with the correct form of the phrasal verbs in the box.

hold on	~~go on~~	look out	show off
show up	go off	shop around	check in

1 Don't stop talking! **Go on** ! I'm listening.

2 I thought they weren't coming, then they _____ at 10:00 P.M.

3 I'm looking for a cheap flight, so I'll have to _____ .

4 He's always talking about how wonderful he is. He's always _____ .

5 My alarm _____ too early this morning.

6 _____ ! The glass is going to fall! Oops! Too late.

7 You want his phone number? _____ a second. I'll get it for you.

8 The first thing to do when you arrive at an airport is _____ .

Pronunciation

9 Weak sounds

To get a natural rhythm in English, some "grammatical" words are often unstressed. Look at the examples in the chart.

Auxiliary verbs	is are was were do did has have would can
Articles	a the
Pronouns	he she it we you they that which
Prepositions	at by for from in of on with

When they are unstressed, they are pronounced with a weak form.

> She's from /frəm/ Mexico.
> Are /ər/ you sure?

🎧 Listen and repeat.

These words are only stressed when used at the end of a sentence, or for emphasis.

Sentence stress

1 The main stress in a phrase or sentence is on key information. <u>Underline</u> the key words in this phone conversation.

> **Assistant** Hello. Callaflight. Can I help you?
> **Customer** Yes, I'm looking for a flight to Tokyo.
> **A** When would you like to travel?
> **C** I was hoping to travel on Friday, at about 9:00 in the morning.
> **A** OK. Do you want to travel from New York?
> **C** Yes, please. If you can make it JFK, that would be great.
> **A** OK … I'm looking at a flight that leaves at 9:40. Would that be all right?
> **C** That would be fine.
> **A** And when were you thinking of returning?
> **C** It's just a one-way I need. Can I pay for it now?
> **A** Sure. Can you give me your credit card details?
> **C** It's a VISA card, number 0494 …

🎧 Listen and check key words.

2 Find the unstressed words in the conversation in exercise 1, and write a /ə/ symbol above them.

3 Practice reading the conversation aloud. You will only have time to repeat the lines if you say the weak sounds naturally!

Listening

10 Interview with a stuntwoman

1 Carla Simpson is a stuntwoman in the movies. Which of the following activities do you think are a regular part of a stuntwoman's job?

- ☑ falling from high buildings
- ☐ driving ambulances
- ☐ using weapons
- ☐ falling off horses
- ☐ acting
- ☐ fire work
- ☐ hand fighting
- ☐ dressing up
- ☐ climbing trees
- ☐ driving

🎧 Listen to the interview with her and check.

2 Answer the questions.
1 Who did the stunts for women in the past?
2 Why are stuntwomen very much in demand these days?
3 Why did Carla's teacher tell her to try stuntwork?
4 What does Carla think is most important in making stunts safe?
5 Why can't they let actors do stunts?
6 What scares Carla the most in life?

3 Complete the lines from the interview with the correct form of the verb in parentheses.

1 … Carla Simpson, who's succeeded in _____ (become) one of Hollywood's top stuntwomen.

2 But of course these days we expect women _____ (do) the stunts…

3 And had you always planned _____ (become) a stuntwoman?

4 … I remember _____ (climb) trees and _____ (jump) off high walls when I was very young.

5 You often get hurt, even on simple stunts, which is why they can't let the actors _____ (do) them.

🎧 Listen again and check.

Vocabulary Crossword 2

Use the clues to complete the crossword. All these words and expressions have appeared in Units 5–8.

ACROSS

1 Scientists are sure we'll _____ life on other planets soon. (8)
5 The mark that stays on your skin after you've cut yourself is a _____ . (4)
9 Andy isn't a real vegetarian – he _____ fish. (4)
11 I love curry – in fact, I like all hot and _____ Indian food. (5)
12 These flowers are gorgeous! Let me find a _____ to put them in. (4)
14 I'll come to the talk on philosophy, but I think it might _____ over my head! (2)
16 Do you wear business or _____ clothes at work? (6)
18 I take these painkillers for any kind of _____ or pain. (4)
19 Mao Zedong came from a very _____ part of China. (6)
21 Does Emma have straight or _____ hair? (5)
23 In Mexico you can lie on the beach and visit ancient _____ in the same day. (5)
24 At the end of a successful performance, the audience will _____ . (4)
26 It was supposed to cost $80, but I got a 10% _____, so I paid $72. (8)
30 A "Would pizza be _____ for dinner?" (2)
   B "Sure, that would be great."
31 I think governments should take stronger action against global warming. But until then, we can each _____ our part. (2)
34 A warranty is a written _____ to replace or repair a product. (9)
35 An elephant's nose is called a _____ . (5)
38 I'm afraid Carol and I just don't see eye _____ eye on most things. (2)
39 If you are unafraid of anything, you are _____ . (8)
40 Harry Potter and the Deathly Hallows _____ out in 2007. (4)
42 Football is called soccer in North America to _____ it from American football. (11)

DOWN

1 A "I'm expecting a baby."
   B "Congratulations! When is it _____ ?" (3)
   A "September."
2 Dan is so excited this week. He _____ off on his around-the-world trip next week. (4)
3 We've spent $150 _____ gas this week! (2)
4 Pam is such a relaxed person—she's really _____ going. (4)
6 I've tried to _____ my phobia of dogs, but I've never had any success. (4)
7 This house is a bit of a ruin, but we're going to _____ it to its original condition. (7)
8 There is always a lot of _____ between teams from the same city. (7)
10 I'd love to have a table in my kitchen, but it would take up too much _____ . (5)
13 Sandra could be a supermodel if she wanted—she's so tall and _____ . (4)
15 "To _____ " means to put a new product on the market. (6)
17 The ad said the views from the hotel would be good – in fact they're absolutely _____! (8)
20 It's very, very small—it's absolutely _____. (4)
22 At 16,500 feet above sea-level you can die from _____ of oxygen. (4)
25 We're going _____ Africa. (2)
27 A _____ is a friendly informal conversation, usually between friends. (4)
28 Busy rich people sometimes employ _____ to look after their children. (7)
29 On your hand you have a thumb, and on your foot you have a big _____ . (3)
31 I have so many _____ and so little money, but I'll have to start paying people back soon. (5)
32 Do you think polar bears will really become _____ during this century? (7)
33 I sleep in a _____ . I'm on top, and my younger sister is underneath. (7)
36 Living to a hundred will _____ the norm within fifty years. (2)
37 Computers are already more powerful than the human _____ . (5)
39 I'll wear anything that _____ me. (4)
41 We eat together _____ a family every evening. (2)

9 It depends how you look at it

Conditionals • *should/could/might have done*
• *make* and *do* • Linking in connected speech

Conditionals

1 Recognizing conditionals

1 Do the quiz. What kind of friend are you?

2 Find examples of these conditional forms from the quiz to complete the chart.

1 *-if* + Present + Present (×2)
If I promise to do something, I do it.

2 *-if* + Present + *will* (×2)

3 *-if* + Past + *would* (×2)

4 *-if* + Past Perfect + *would have* (×2)

What kind of friend are you?

1 **You say to a friend, "I'll give you a call tomorrow." But do you?**
 a Yes. If I promise to do something, I do it.
 b No. I didn't mean it. It was just a way of saying good-bye.

2 **You get a text from a friend. Do you reply immediately?**
 a Yes. If a friend gets in touch with me, I always reply.
 b It depends. If I have something to say, I'll text back.

3 **Your friend has bought a dress which she really likes, but you think it is awful. What do you say?**
 a If she likes it, I'll tell her it looks good. It doesn't matter what I think.
 b I tell her the truth. That's what friends are for.

4 **A friend says to you, "If anyone asks where I was last night, say I was with you." Would you lie for your friend?**
 a If it was really important, I'd lie. But I'd want to know what it was all about.
 b This sounds like it could be something nasty or illegal. No, I wouldn't.

5 **Your friend tells you a secret and makes you swear not to tell anyone. Do you?**
 a Of course not. A promise is a promise.
 b If it was really juicy, of course I'd tell other people! How could I keep it to myself?

6 **Your friend left her cell phone at your house, so you read her messages and found out that she'd been saying horrible things about you. What would you have done?**
 a If she'd left her phone anywhere, I wouldn't have looked at her messages. They're private.
 b If she hadn't wanted me to read her messages, she wouldn't have left her phone. You can't blame me for being nosy!

QUIZ ANSWERS

Mainly **A**s: You're a true, loyal friend. You really believe that a friend in need is a friend indeed. You would do anything for your friends.

Mainly **B**s: You sometimes put yourself before your friends. You're a bit of a fair-weather friend. Who would want to have you as their best friend?

2 Types of conditional

Match the lines in the charts to make conditional sentences.

No condition (zero conditionals)

present	+	present
Jenny never says thank you	if	you don't keep it in a fridge?
Henry always gets angry		you criticize him.
Does meat go bad		you do something for her.

Possible conditions (first conditional)

will	+	present
I'll help you	if	I go gray and get wrinkles?
Things will get better		you just wait and are patient.
Will you still love me		I have time.

Improbable conditions (second conditional)

would	+	past
I wouldn't do that	if	people smiled more.
The world would be a happier place		I were you.
What would you do		you saw a fight on the street?

Impossible conditions (third conditional)

would have	+	past perfect
I wouldn't have cooked meat	if	you hadn't had enough money?
The Lakers would have won		you'd told me you were vegetarian.
Would you have gone to college		the Knicks hadn't scored in the last minute.

Possible conditions

3 *if + will / might / must / should*

Match a line in **A** with a line in **B**.

A		B	
1	☐ If I'm going to be late,	a	we might go skiing this winter. We'll see.
2	☐ If Tony calls,	b	I'll give you a call and let you know.
3	☐ If you don't feel well,	c	you'll have to do some exercise.
4	☐ If you're ever in Boston,	d	tell him I'm out, and I'll call him later.
5	☐ If we can afford it,	e	turn everything off and start again.
6	☐ If you want to stay in shape,	f	you should go to bed and get some rest.
7	☐ If your computer doesn't work,	g	they won't grow, they'll die.
8	☐ If you don't water your flowers,	h	you must come and visit me.

Improbable conditions

4 What would you do?

1 Read Social Dilemmas 1–7. Put the verbs in parentheses in the correct form.

What would you do if …

1 you **_found_** (find) a wallet with $20 in it and no name inside?

2 you _____ (find) a wallet with $10,000 in it and the name of a well-known millionaire?

3 a friend _____ (cheat) on a school exam and got a better grade than you?

4 a work colleague, who was poor, _____ (claim) expenses that you knew were false?

5 a teenage girl you know _____ (get) too involved in an online relationship?

6 you _____ (take) a photo of a celebrity doing something she shouldn't, and she asked you not to give it to the papers?

7 your friend _____ (ask) you to lie to her parents so she could go out with a boy?

2 Read the responses. Put the verbs in parentheses in the correct form.

a _**I'd tell**_ (tell) her to stop all contact with him. If she _____ (not be) careful, she _____ (can) get into a lot of trouble.

b I _____ (ignore) it. Everyone fiddles their expenses.

c I _____ (tell) her that I wasn't happy, but if she _____ (be) my best friend, I _____ (lie) for her.

d I _____ (keep) it. It's not that much money. How _____ (can) I find the owner?

e I _____ (get) in touch with a newspaper, and I _____ (sell) the photo for as much as possible. I _____ (not care) what she thought.

f I _____ (not give) it back even if I _____ (know) the owner. He's rich. He _____ (not miss) $10,000. For him, that's nothing.

g I don't know what I _____ (do). I _____ (not like) to tell the teachers, but if they _____ (be) important exams, I _____ (be) really angry.

3 Match the responses to the social dilemmas.

1 ☐ **d**   2 ☐   3 ☐   4 ☐   5 ☐   6 ☐   7 ☐

Impossible conditions

5 Life-changing decisions

Read the texts. Write sentences in the third conditional using the prompts.

Laura's life Laura majored in economics at a university in New York. She couldn't find work in New York, so she accepted a job working in a bank in Boston. She went out with a man named Mike, who loved her very much, but she knew he wasn't the man for her. Then she met Bruce, fell in love, got married, and had two kids, Bill and Maddox.

1 If / Laura / not study / economics / not get / job.

If Laura hadn't studied economics, she wouldn't have gotten the job.

2 If / find / job / New York / not go / Boston.

_____

3 If / marry / Mike / not meet / Bruce.

_____

4 If / not marry / Bruce / not have / Bill and Maddox.

_____

Mark's life Everything changed for Mark when he went on vacation to the Virgin Islands five years ago. Mark had a very stressful job as a corporate lawyer in Cleveland, Ohio. On his first day of vacation, he was checking his email constantly, but on his second day, he decided to take a surfing lesson. Mark's instructor, Jimmy, showed him around the islands and reminded him of the importance of relaxation and fun. In fact, Mark decided not to return to Ohio. Instead, he used his savings to open a surf shop near the beach.

5 If / Mark / stay in Cleveland / not give up his job

_____

6 If / not take / the surfing lesson / not meet / Jimmy

_____

7 If / continue / check email / have / stressful vacation

_____

8 If / not have / savings / not be able / open a business

_____

6 Questions and answers

Write questions and answers about what people didn't do!

1 **A** It's a shame. I never went to college.
   B <u>What would you have studied?</u>
   A <u>I'd have studied psychology</u> . (psychology)

2 **A** I didn't travel much in my life. I didn't have the chance.
   B Where _____ ?
   A _____ . (Africa)

3 **A** I didn't win the lottery, so I didn't buy a new car.
   B What kind _____ ?
   A _____ . (a Mercedes)

4 **A** I saw Tom Hanks in a restaurant. I wish I'd spoken to him.
   B _____ said to him?
   A _____ told _____ . (he was a great actor)

5 **A** Oof! I'm too full to eat a dessert.
   B _____ had?
   A _____ . (chocolate cake)

6 **A** We had daughters. We never had a son.
   B _____ called him?
   A We _____ . (Robert)

7 **A** I always wanted a large family.
   B How many children _____ liked?
   A _____ . (six)

8 **A** I don't think you should have taken I-95. Big mistake!
   B Which road _____ ?
   A _____ . (US 301)

should / might / could have done

7 Past possibilities

Complete the sentences with a phrase from the box and the correct form of the verb in parentheses.

could have	should have	shouldn't have	wouldn't have

1 James <u>could have been</u> (be) a professional football player, but he broke his leg.

2 You _____ (tell) me the truth. I hate it when people lie to me.

3 They didn't invite me to their wedding, but I _____ (go) even if they had. He's all right, but I don't like her at all.

4 Stop using your cell phone while you're driving. You nearly hit that car! You _____ (kill) us all!

5 Sorry, I've forgotten your address. I _____ (write) it down. What was it again?

6 A present! For me! That's so nice! You _____ (bother), really!

8 Advice about the past

Give advice using *should have* or *shouldn't have*.

1 I told her I thought she was weak and selfish.
    <u>You shouldn't have said that. You know she's very sensitive.</u>

2 I drove past your house last night.
    _____ come in and said hello! I was home.

3 I stole some money from my mother's purse.
    _____ . That's so bad!

4 I'm absolutely broke. I don't have a penny!
    _____ so many clothes. You didn't need them.

5 There's a police car behind me.
    _____ through those red lights. That was really silly.

Pronunciation

9 Linking in connected speech (1)

Word-linking is very important if you want to speak fluently.

1 Any word that begins with a vowel sound links with the word before it.

you'd ‿ asked /yədæskt/	about ‿ it /əbaʊtɪt/
she'd ‿ have /ʃidəv/	explained ‿ it /ɪkspleɪndɪt/

2 Two vowel sounds link using the sounds /w/ or /y/.

to ‿ us /tʊwəs/	she ‿ asked /ʃiyɑskt/

🎧 Listen and repeat.

▶▶ **Phonetic Symbols p. 93**

3 There are many links in the whole sentence.

> If you'd ‿ asked ‿ her ‿ about ‿ it, she'd ‿ have ‿ explained ‿ it ‿ all to ‿ us.

🎧 Listen and repeat the parts of the sentence you hear, until you can say the whole sentence.

Read these sentences aloud marking the linking between groups of words.

1 He could have gone home.

2 She might have left early.

3 I should have written it down.

4 We shouldn't have spent all our money.

5 If they'd seen him, they'd have told him.

6 She wouldn't have gotten the job if she hadn't passed her exam.

🎧 Listen and check.

Verbs forms for unreal situations

10 *What a mistake!*

Rewrite the sentences using the words in parentheses.

■ You've got that wrong

A man who robbed a convenience store in Iowa came back to retrieve his wallet, which he'd accidentally left behind. He found the store clerk on the phone describing him to the police and started correcting the facts. "He's about 5ft 10in," the store clerk was saying. "I'm 6ft 2in," the suspect complained. "And about 38 years old," the store clerk continued. "I'm 34," protested the suspect. A deputy sheriff arrived moments later to arrest him.

1 He forgot his wallet. He went back to the store. (if)

_____

2 He went back to the store. He didn't escape. (if / might)

_____

3 He started correcting the shopkeeper. (should)

_____

■ Big bang

Thieves in Kuala Lumpur broke into an office and found the safe, which was holding $50,000. They used dynamite to blow the safe but only succeeded in destroying the whole seven-story building. The safe was left intact. Fortunately, no one was injured.

4 They didn't open the safe. They didn't escape with $50,000. (if)

_____

5 They used too much dynamite. (should)

_____

6 It was possible that they killed themselves. (could)

_____

■ How does it work?

Three teenagers attempted to steal a woman's car at gunpoint outside of her home in Seattle as she was removing something from the trunk. She gave them the keys calmly, but when the boys got into the car, they couldn't figure out how to start it. They had no choice but to abandon the car. Unfortunately for them, the surveillance camera at a nearby business videoed the boys as they ran away from the scene. Fortunately for the woman, they left the keys in the ignition.

7 Because the woman was removing something from the trunk, she didn't see the boys. (if not / might)

_____

8 The boys didn't check for cameras in the street. (should)

_____

9 The boys didn't steal the car because they didn't know how to start it. (would / if)

_____

■ A robber with problems

An unfortunate bank robber in Miami had just finished filling his bag with cash when he put his gun in his pocket too hastily and shot himself in the leg. As he staggered towards his getaway car, he tripped on the pavement and knocked out two of his gold teeth. After struggling to his feet, he crossed the road and was run down by a van. Police are looking for a man with a bullet in his leg, two missing teeth, and serious head wounds.

10 It was possible that he killed a passer-by. (could)

_____

11 He tripped. He knocked out two teeth. (if)

_____

12 He didn't look where he was going. (should)

_____

Vocabulary

11 make and do

1 Which expressions go with *make*, and which go with *do*? Write them in the correct columns.

a mistake	up your mind	the shopping
a decision	a mess	someone a favor
sure (that)	the housework	nothing
my best	a speech	a profit
exercises	a noise	a phone call
friends with	the dishes	progress

make	do

2 Complete the sentences using the correct form of the expressions from exercise 1.

1 First she said yes, then she said no, but in the end she _____ to marry him.

2 I like to stay in shape, so I _____ every day.

3 I love Sundays! I can lie on the sofa all day and _____.

4 Shh! Don't _____. The baby's asleep.

5 My teacher says I must work harder, but I can't work any harder, I'm _____.

6 We have an agreement in our house. I cook dinner every evening, and afterwards James _____.

7 Could you _____ please? Could you give me a ride to the airport?

8 We have some nice new neighbors. We've already _____ them.

9 Is there a public phone booth near here? I have to _____.

10 Before you go on vacation you should _____ all the doors and windows are locked.

Listening

12 Scams

1 "Scams" or "cons" are ways of tricking people to get money out of them. Read the leaflet warning people about common scams.

SCAM WATCH!

Watch out for these common scams

1 Your phone rings. When you answer it, the caller checks your name and then tells you that you've won a prize. They ask you to call another number to claim the prize. When you dial the number, they say you will have to pay $50 to get the prize.

2 You receive a fake e-mail, which looks like it's come from your bank, telling you that your security details need to be updated. The e-mail sends you to a website that looks just like your bank's. The website gives you some new security details for your account.

3 A thief steals your credit card without you knowing. He/She then calls you and pretends to be from the police, saying that they've just stopped someone trying to use your card. They ask you for your PIN number.

🎧 Listen to Peter and Elaine talking about the scams. Correct any details that are wrong in the leaflet.

2 🎧 Listen again and complete the lines from the conversation.

1 Apparently if you _____ back, the prizes _____ worthless, but they _____ you as much as $50 for the call.

2 Mmm, I must admit, I _____ for that.

3 It's obvious a bank _____ for his PIN number, but you _____ that at the time, _____ you?

4 I mean, if they _____ that one on me now, at least I _____ about it.

5 But honestly, if we _____ not careful, we _____ being suspicious of everyone.

10 All things high tech

Noun phrases • Articles and possessives • *all/every, myself/each other*
• *a suitcase/luggage* • Phrasal verb + noun • Diphthongs

Noun phrases

1 The low-cost laptop

Complete the text about the XO laptop using noun phrases a–o.

a	**the** organization's founder
b	**every** child in **the** world ✓
c	**the** dust and **the** heat
d	**all** over **the** world
e	one watt of power
f	**a** range of
g	he saw for **himself**
h	**the** most hard-wearing computer
i	with **each other**
j	viewed in bright sunlight
k	children's lives
l	**a** big problem
m	50% of **the** world's population
n	**a single** battery
o	**their** own laptop

Low-cost laptops
for the world's children

One Laptop Per Child (OLPC), a non-profit organization, is the creator of the XO laptop, a low-cost computer designed to give (1) **b** access to knowledge and education.

Nicholas Negraponte, (2) ▢, wanted children from (3) ▢ to be equipped with the latest technology. It was while he was on a trip to a Cambodian village that (4) ▢ how access to the Internet could change (5) ▢.

There is no single electricity supply throughout the world, so power is (6) ▢. The XO computer can be powered in several ways, including a pull cord and a solar panel. It uses less than (7) ▢ and can operate for more than 12 hours using (8) ▢.

The latest model comes with a touchscreen, 5 GHz Wifi, and Bluetooth technology. It has both a color and monochrome display so that it can be (9) ▢. Users are able to share data (10) ▢ easily.

The laptop is more flexible and (11) ▢ ever designed. It is engineered to withstand the harsh environmental conditions found in developing countries – from (12) ▢ of the Libyan desert to the daily downpours of the Brazilian rainforests.

There is a brightly-colored XO logo on the back. Children can select from (13) ▢ colors so they can easily identify (14) ▢ in a crowded classroom.

The XO is the first of many cheap laptops that aim to enable (15) ▢ to have cheap Internet access in the future.

Indefinite article: *a/an*

2 Saying what something or somebody is

What are these things?

1 A Dell <u>is a computer.</u>
2 Apple Macs and HPs <u>are computers.</u>
3 A Boeing 747 _____
4 Jets and gliders _____
5 A Mini Cooper _____
6 BMWs and Toyotas _____
7 A Samsung Galaxy _____
8 Motorola Droids and Apple iPhones _____

Who were these people?

9 Einstein <u>was a scientist.</u>
10 Newton and Pasteur _____
11 Van Gogh _____
12 Picasso and Monet _____
13 Charles Dickens _____
14 Proust and Tolstoy _____

Put *a* or *an* into the gaps.

15 My daughter's <u>an</u> actor.
16 I'm _____ optimist.
17 Jane is _____ good painter.
18 Jack's _____ interesting person.
19 When I was _____ child, I was afraid of dogs.
20 Peter's _____ idiot. He knows nothing.

Definite article: *the*

3 You know the one I mean

Complete the sentences with words from the boxes.

~~the environment~~	the sky	the beach
the government	the country	the future
the mountains	the weather	

1 We need to protect <u>the environment</u>. We pollute it daily.
2 I used to live in _____. Now I live in the city.
3 How many stars are there in _____?
4 No one can see into _____. Who knows what will happen?
5 I love taking my kids to _____. We go paddling and build sandcastles.
6 We go climbing in _____.
7 She's a federal employee. She works for _____.
8 People talk about _____ because our climate is fascinating.

~~the doctor~~	the post office	the door
the salt	the garden	the radio
the bathroom	the library	

9 That's a nasty cough. You should see <u>the doctor</u>.
10 Pass me _____. It's next to the pepper.
11 Close _____. It's freezing in here.
12 I go to _____ once a week. I love books.
13 Let's sit in _____. It's such a nice day.
14 I'm going to _____. Do you want me to mail your letters?
15 "Where's Ana?"

"She's in _____ taking a shower."
16 I don't watch TV much, but I like listening to

_____.

~~the best student~~	the most delicious
the same	the first

17 Pablo is <u>the best student</u> in the class.
18 I'll have _____ pizza as you—cheese and tomato.
19 This is _____ time I've been in love.
20 That was _____ ice cream I've ever had in my life.

No article

4 Things in general

1 Match a line in **A** with a line in **B**.

A		B	
1	☐ Apples ...	a	is full of vitamins.
2	☐ Fruit ...	b	doesn't lead to happiness.
3	☐ Bees ...	c	grow on trees.
4	☐ Money ...	d	are stronger than women.
5	☐ Men ...	e	are less mature than girls.
6	☐ Boys ...	f	make honey.

2 Complete these English proverbs with a noun from the box.

~~beauty~~　love　variety　time　honesty　crime

1 _Beauty_ is in the eye of the beholder.
2 _____ is the best policy.
3 All's fair in _____ and war.
4 _____ is the spice of life.
5 _____ doesn't pay.
6 _____ heals all wounds.

3 Complete the sentences with a game or academic subject.

~~psychology~~　biology　poker　chess

1 James is studying _psychology_ at school.
2 _____ is a game of strategy played on a black and white board.
3 _____ is the study of plants and animals.
4 I love playing _____, but I hate losing money.

5 Article or no article?

Complete the sentences with *the* or nothing (–).

Everyday places

1 I go to __–__ school at 8:00. The school is in _____ center of _____ town.

2 My dad's at _____ work. He teaches _____ children and adults.

3 I'm going _____ home now. I'm tired. I'll be at _____ home tomorrow.

4 Good night. I'm going to _____ bed now. Jane's in _____ bed already.

5 My brother's studying _____ Math at _____ Indiana University. My sister's at _____ University of Illinois.

Place names

6 We're staying at __the__ Pierre Hotel on _____ Fifth Avenue.

7 We can see _____ Central Park, _____ St. Patrick's Cathedral, and _____ Chrysler Building from our room.

8 We're going to eat at _____ Palm Tree Restaurant. We used to go to _____ Giovanni's Restaurant until it closed down.

9 I want to see _____ Bronx Zoo, _____ Guggenheim, and _____ Grand Central Station.

10 Last year we went on vacation to _____ Mediterranean. We met people from _____ Mexico, _____ Japan, and _____ Middle East.

Meals

11 What did you have for __–__ lunch?

12 Where should we have _____ dinner?

13 What time do you want _____ breakfast?

Transportation

14 I usually go to work by __–__ bus, but this morning _____ bus was late, so I missed my meeting.

15 I go everywhere by _____ train. I never travel by _____ plane. _____ last plane I took was in 2003.

Nationalities

16 __The__ French love food, but only French food.

17 _____ Italian people have great style.

18 _____ Mexicans are proud of their heritage.

Possessives

6 *my* and *mine*

1 Complete the chart.

Possessive adjective	Possessive pronoun
my	mine
your	_____
her	_____
_____	his
its	_____
_____	ours
their	_____

2 Complete the sentences with a possessive adjective or a possessive pronoun.

1 Why are you taking __my__ car? What's wrong with _____?

2 Pat and Peter's house is nice, but we prefer __yours__. _____ house is bigger than _____.

3 My sister is always taking _____ clothes without asking me. I never take _____. I wish she'd learn that what's mine is _____ and what's hers is _____.

4 Let me introduce you to Mike. He's an old friend of _____. We were at school together.

5 Tim bakes _____ own bread, and Kim makes _____ own jam.

6 The *TJB Bank* has changed _____ name to the *Allied Friendly*.

7 Apostrophe *'s* and *s'*

Write the apostrophes in the correct place.

1 This is Jack's brother, Tommy.

2 What is your mothers maiden name?

3 Childrens clothes are so expensive.

4 Jenny is my brothers girlfriend.

5 Our neighbors children make a lot of noise.

6 Bill and Sues dog is a retriever.

7 I'm going to Adrianas house tonight.

8 Have you seen yesterdays newspaper?

9 I'm having two weeks vacation.

10 Here is tomorrows weather.

all and *every*

8 Position of *all*

Write the word *all* in the correct place in the sentences.

1 In my family we all like baseball.

2 I've spent day on the computer.

3 I've done my homework.

4 Pedro's invited the whole class to his house—of us!

5 I need is a pair of socks.

6 I've wanted to meet you my life.

7 I like kinds of music from classical to jazz to rock.

9 *all/every/everyone*

Complete the sentences with a word in the box.

all	every	everyone	everything	everywhere

1 The police searched __every__ room.

2 _____ your car needs is some gas.

3 It was a great party. _____ had a wonderful time. _____ the food was eaten.

4 Burglars emptied my apartment. They took _____.

5 I believe _____ word he says.

6 It's been raining _____ week.

7 You must tell me _____ about your trip.

8 I've spent _____ penny I have. I mean *had*.

Pronouns

10 *myself/each other*

Complete the sentences with a reflexive pronoun (*myself, yourself,* etc) or *each other*.

1 I hurt __myself__ climbing a tree.

2 You should drive more slowly. You could kill _____ if you aren't careful.

3 My children are too young to look after _____.

4 Bye, kids! I hope you enjoy _____ at the party.

5 How long have you two known _____?

6 My mother and I are very close. We speak to _____ on the phone every day.

7 Selfish people only care about _____.

8 I behaved very badly. I'm ashamed of _____.

Vocabulary

11 *a suitcase / luggage*

1 Match a count noun in **A** with a non-count noun in **B**.

A count	B uncount
1 ☐ a suitcase	a fruit
2 ☐ a loaf	b luggage
3 ☐ a job	c work
4 ☐ a suggestion	d advice
5 ☐ an apple	e travel
6 ☐ a trip	f bread

2 Are these words countable (C) or non-countable (N)?

1 **N** news   3 ☐ information

2 ☐ homework   4 ☐ furniture

3 Correct the mistakes in these sentences.

1 Can you give me ~~an~~ *some* information about train times?

2 I'd like a sliced white ~~bread~~ *loaf*, please.

3 How many luggage do you have?

4 The news are always very depressing.

5 He gave me a very good advice.

6 I have a lot of homeworks tonight.

7 I'd like some fruits for breakfast.

8 I'm exhausted. The travel was very long and tiring.

9 She has a very good work in the city.

10 I bought all my furnitures second hand.

4 Choose the correct words.

1 People say that *travel / trip* broadens the mind.

2 Could you give me *an advice / a suggestion*?

3 Don't forget to buy *some bread / some loaf* at the store.

4 I'm looking for *job / work* in marketing.

5 What *a lovely weather / lovely weather* we're having!

6 To get a job you need *experience / experiences*.

7 There *'s too much traffic / are too many traffics* in New York.

8 What's on TV? Do you have *a paper / some paper*?

9 *How many times / How much time* have you been to Seoul?

10 *How many times / How much time* do you spend watching TV?

Pronunciation

12 Diphthongs

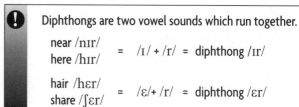

❗	Diphthongs are two vowel sounds which run together.

near /nɪr/
here /hɪr/   =   /ɪ/ + /r/   = diphthong /ɪr/

hair /hɛr/
share /ʃɛr/   =   /ɛ/ + /r/   = diphthong /ɛr/

▶▶ **Phonetic Symbols p. 93**

1 Write the words from the box next to the correct diphthong.

where	clear	stay	shy	know	sure
now	phone	high	enjoy	poor	deer
aloud	noise	bear	weigh		

1 /ɪr/ = /ɪ/ + /r/   here _____ _____

2 /ɛr/ = /ɛ/ + /r/   hair _____ _____

3 /eɪ/ = /e/ + /ɪ/   pay _____ _____

4 /oʊ/ = /o/ + /ʊ/   go _____ _____

5 /aɪ/ = /a/ + /ɪ/   my _____ _____

6 /ɔɪ/ = /ɔ/ + /ɪ/   boy _____ _____

7 /aʊ/ = /a/ + /ʊ/   how _____ _____

8 /ʊr/ = /ʊ/ + /r/   tour _____

🎧 Listen and check.

2 Transcribe the words in the sentences in phonetic script. They are all diphthongs.

1 We caught the /pleɪn/ _____ to the /saʊθ/ _____ of /speɪn/_____ .

2 The /bɔɪ/ _____ in the red /koʊt/ _____ said that he /ɪnˈdʒɔɪd/ _____ the trip.

3 I've /noʊn/ _____ Sue for /ˈnɪrli/ _____ /faɪv/ _____ years.

4 She's /ˈwɛrɪŋ/ _____ a red /roʊz/ _____ in her /hɛr/_____ .

5 Not many people /smoʊk/ _____ /paɪps/ _____ these /deɪz/_____ .

6 He /laɪks/ _____ to /raɪd/ _____ a big black /ˈmoʊtərˌsaɪkl/_____ .

🎧 Listen and check.

He likes to ride a big black motorcycle.

Phrasal verbs

13 Phrasal verb + noun (2)

1 Match a phrasal verb in **A** with a noun in **B**.

A		B	
1 ☐ apply for		a	a new apartment
2 ☐ run out of		b	a job
3 ☐ clean up		c	an old building
4 ☐ move into		d	your computer
5 ☐ knock down		e	milk
6 ☐ plug in		f	a mess

2 Complete the sentences with the correct form of the phrasal verbs from exercise 1.

1 We've __run__ __out__ __of__ sugar. I'll buy some at the store.

2 When are you _____ _____ your new house?

3 The kitchen is a disaster! Why can't you _____ _____ your mess after you've been cooking?

4 I _____ _____ a job I saw advertised on the Internet.

5 If your computer stops working, unplug everything, then _____ it _____ again.

6 Did you see? They _____ _____ the old theater to build a new apartment building.

3 Match a phrasal verb in **A** with a noun in **B**.

A		B	
1 ☐ sort out		a	an illness
2 ☐ get over		b	a problem
3 ☐ work out		c	the answer
4 ☐ let down		d	your friends
5 ☐ put out		e	the money you owe
6 ☐ pay back		f	a fire

4 Complete the sentences with the correct form of the phrasal verbs from exercise 3.

1 You promised that you'd help me, and now you won't. You've really _____ me _____ .

2 May I borrow $10? I'll _____ you _____ tomorrow.

3 I've had the flu for about a week, and I'm only just _____ _____ it.

4 "The washing machine's broken, and I'm late for work." "Don't worry. I'll _____ everything _____."

5 The firemen arrived very quickly, but they couldn't _____ _____ the fire, and the house burned down.

6 What's 15% of 2,500? I can't _____ it _____ in my head.

Listening

14 Lost and found

1 Which of these items do you think are most often left behind on public transportation? Number them 1–5.

☐ glasses
☐ bags
☐ coats and jackets
☐ umbrellas
☐ cell phones

🎧 Listen to two colleagues, Mark and Amy, talking about lost property and check.

2 Choose the correct answer.

1 Amy is annoyed about losing her umbrella because it was

   a new. **b** very expensive. **c** of high quality.

2 The bags that people most often leave behind on buses and trains are

   a designer bags. **b** shopping bags. **c** handbags.

3 At first, people who call their lost cell phones are

   a rude. **b** thieves. **c** very grateful.

4 People often leave their laptops

   a in taxis.
   b on airport X-ray machines.
   c in airport departure gates.

5 Most people who leave their laptops behind

   a don't realize they've lost them.
   b don't have time to contact Lost and Found.
   c think that someone must have stolen them.

3 🎧 Listen again. Complete Amy's description of her umbrella.

> " Actually it's a very _____ umbrella _____ . It's _____ — it _____ a golfing umbrella. And it _____ down the side of it. "

11 Seeing is believing

Modal verbs of probability • Continuous infinitive
• Prepositions – verb + prepositions • Word formation
• Linking in connected speech

Modal verbs of probability – present

1 must/could/might/can't

1 *Ask Ruth* is a problem page in a magazine. Read Ruth's reply to Luke Basset. What is his problem?

2 Complete the deductions about Luke with the modal verb of probability from the box.

must have (x 2)	~~must be~~	can't have
might not know	may get annoyed	could be jealous
may be studying		

1 Luke **must be** the eldest child in the family.
2 He _____ a younger brother named Cal.
3 Luke's friends _____ with Cal.
4 Luke's parents _____ very demanding jobs.
5 Luke _____ for some exams.
6 The parents _____ that Cal has problems at school.
7 Luke _____ of Cal.
8 Cal _____ many friends.

3 Read about Jane Iverson. What is her problem?

4 (Circle) the correct modal verb of probability in the sentences about Jane and the Fletchers.

1 The Fletchers *must be / can't be* Jane's neighbors.
2 Jane *must have / may have* three sons.
3 The Fletchers *can't be / could be* a retired couple.
4 Jane *must know / might know* about a law.
5 Jane *may be / can't be* thinking of consulting a lawyer.
6 The Fletchers *must have / can't have* children of their own living at home.

Read the original letters on page 88.

QUESTION:
Dear Ruth,
We fight all the time. I hate him! …
Luke Basset

RUTH SAYS:
Dear Luke,

It is very difficult not to get angry with your brother in your situation. At your age you need time on your own and some privacy when you are with your friends. Ask your parents to find time in their busy lives to sit down and talk to you about what is happening. Tell them how Cal is stopping you from doing your schoolwork. The youngest child in a family is often given special treatment and gets very spoiled. Also, you should tell them about the problems Cal is having at school. He won't leave you alone until he has more friends of his own.

Yours, *Ruth*

QUESTION:
Dear Ruth,
We live in the house of our dreams.
We don't want to move but we're going crazy. …
Jane Iverson

RUTH SAYS:
Dear Jane,

When people live side by side they need to be tolerant of each other's way of life. Your children need their sleep, and you have every right to enjoy your beautiful backyard. Try talking to the Fletchers again, promise that your sons will make less noise during the day if they make less noise in the evenings. Also, you are right, there may be a law controlling the height of garden hedges. However, going to court is expensive. It's in both your interests to sort out the problem yourselves.

Yours, *Ruth*

2 Matching lines

Match a line in **A** with a line in **B**.

A	B
1 ☐ You can't be hungry.	a They have nothing in common.
2 ☐ She must be out.	b They've been holding hands all evening.
3 ☐ He can't be American	c There aren't any lights on in her apartment.
4 ☐ You must be very happy	d Nobody pays $1,000 for a pair of jeans.
5 ☐ They must be tired.	e with your excellent exam results.
6 ☐ They must know each other well.	f We've just had breakfast.
7 ☐ You must be joking!	g They've been traveling all night.
8 ☐ They can't be getting married!	h with an accent like that.

3 Why is he late?

1 Mario is always on time for class, but today he is late. Suggest reasons using *must, might, could,* or *may*.

1 Is he still in bed? (might)

   He might still be in bed.

2 Is he sick? (must)

   _____

3 Is he in the coffee shop? (could)

   _____

4 Does he have a doctor's appointment? (might)

   _____

5 Is he stuck in a traffic jam? (may)

   _____

6 Is his bus late? (might)

   _____

7 Is he talking to a friend from another class? (may)

   _____

8 Does he want to miss the test? (must)

   _____

2 Rewrite the sentences in exercise 1 with *can't*.

1 **He can't be still in bed.**

2 _____

3 _____

4 _____

5 _____

6 _____

7 _____

8 _____

Pronunciation

4 Linking in connected speech (2)

> **!** When *have* is used as an auxiliary verb, it is unstressed. The "h" is not pronounced and the weak form is used /əv/. It is linked with the word before it.
>
> You should have /ʃʊdəv/ eaten breakfast this morning.
>
> When *have* is a full verb, it is stressed. The "h" is pronounced and the strong form is used /hæv/. It cannot be linked with the word before it.
>
> You should have /ʃʊd hæv/ breakfast before you leave.

▶▶ **Phonetic Symbols p. 93**

🎧 Listen and repeat.

Mark the /ə/ sound and the link on *have* in one sentence in each pair. Read the sentences aloud.

1 **a** He must have won the lottery.

   b He must have a lot of money.

2 **a** He might have written it down.

   b He might have a pen you can borrow.

3 **a** You should have let me cut your hair!

   b You should have a proper haircut.

4 **a** You could have a break soon.

   b You could have broken something!

Continuous Infinitive

5 Conversations

Complete the conversations with a suitable verb in the Continuous Infinitive.

1 **A** Do you know where Ben is?

   B I'm not sure. He may __be playing__ games on the computer.

2 **A** Where's Maho?

   B She's upstairs. She must _____ to music in her room.

   A She's not in her room.

   B Try the bathroom. She might _____ a shower.

3 **A** I can't find the thing that changes the TV channel.

   B The remote control? Stand up. You could _____ on it.

4 **A** Have you seen the newspaper?

   B I think James may _____ it.

5 **A** What's that noise?

   B It sounds like an ambulance. It must _____ someone to the hospital.

6 **A** Look over there! It's Mariana and Alex.

   B She can't _____ his hand. She doesn't like him.

   A They must _____ out together. I don't believe it!

7 **A** What's happening outside?

   B It sounds like workers. They must _____ up the road outside.

   A What for?

   B I don't know. They could _____ a broken water pipe.

🎧 Listen and check.

72   Unit 11 • Seeing is believing

Modal verbs of probability – past

6 *must have / might have / may have / can't have*

Look at the pictures. Make deductions about what has probably happened. Write sentences.

1
- must / accident
- might / snowboarding

_____

_____

2
- must / argument
- can't / enjoy / meal

_____

_____

3
- can't / driving test
- may / nervous

_____

_____

4

- could / eat / bird
- bird / might / escape

_____
_____

5

- must / miss / plane
- plane / could / delayed

_____
_____

6

- can't / enjoy / movie
- must / boring

_____
_____

7

- must / cell phone
- might / stolen

_____
_____

8

- must / receive / good news
- may / lottery

_____
_____

7 Rewriting sentences

Rewrite these sentences using the modal verb in parentheses.

1 I'm sure they've arrived. I can hear a car. (must)
   They must have arrived. I can hear a car.

2 I'm sure you didn't study hard for your exams. (couldn't)

   _____

3 Perhaps I left my cell in the Internet cafe. (might)

   _____

4 He has probably been on a diet. (must)

   _____

5 It's possible that they got married in secret. (could)

   _____

6 Perhaps he called while we were out. (may)

   _____

Tense review

8 It's hard to believe

1 Read the first article. Answer the questions.

1 How did Jorge discover his real twin brother?
2 What discovery did Jorge make on Facebook?
3 How was William and Wilber's childhood different from Jorge and Carlos's?

2 Here are some sentences about Jorge's experience. Rewrite them using the words in parentheses.

1 I expect it was strange for the four men to meet each other. (must)

   It must have been strange for the four men to meet each other.

2 I'm sure Jorge's coworker didn't believe her eyes when she saw William working in the butcher shop. (can't)

   _____

3 I don't think the mothers knew that they had the wrong baby. (couldn't)

   _____

4 Perhaps it was difficult for William to go to college because he lived in Santander. (might)

   _____

5 I'm sure Carlos was shocked when Jorge told him about the mix-up. (must)

   _____

3 Read the second article on page 75. Answer the questions.

1 What was Arnie doing when he disappeared?
2 When did the family get Lucky?
3 What was Arnie like when he returned?

4 Here are some sentences about Arnie's story. Rewrite them using the words in parentheses.

1 Perhaps Arnie was stolen by a dog breeder. (might)

   _____

2 Arnie is probably a pedigree dog. (could)

   _____

3 I don't think the family expected Arnie to return. (couldn't)

   _____

4 I'm sure the family were surprised to hear from the neighbor. (must)

   _____

5 Lucky is possibly a mixed-breed dog. (may)

   _____

Identical twins mixed up at birth reunite

Jorge, 24, a designer at an engineering company in Bogotá, couldn't believe his eyes when his coworker showed him a photo of a young butcher she had met at a local butcher shop. The butcher's name was William and he looked just like Jorge! Jorge was even more surprised when he looked at William's Facebook profile and saw several photos of him with another young man who was the image of Jorge's own brother, Carlos. What was going on?

Jorge and Carlos, now an accountant, were raised as fraternal twins in Bogotá. Meanwhile, William and his brother Wilber (the young man in the photos) were raised in the rural town of Santander also as fraternal twins.

So what had happened? Clearly the boys had grown up with the wrong twin. No one knows exactly how this mix-up happened, but it was almost certainly at a hospital in Bogotá. Jorge and his identical twin William were born there, and Carlos, Wilbur's identical twin, had been brought to the hospital from Santander because of health problems after a premature birth.

The four brothers eventually arranged to meet. It has been interesting, but even though William is Jorge's identical twin, and they get along very well, Jorge still considers Carlos to be his true brother.

Arnie the terrier finds his way home after two years

A Tibetan terrier named Arnie, who was missing for nearly two years, has made his way home to his delighted family.

Eleven-year-old Arnie disappeared from his home 21 months ago. His owner, Gillian Singleton, believes he was probably stolen for breeding purposes. "One minute he was playing in the backyard, the next minute he was gone."

Her children David, 9, and Emily, 6, were very upset. The family immediately began a full-scale search for him, but he was nowhere to be found.

As the months passed, they thought Arnie had gone forever. They took in a stray dog, named Lucky, and cared for him.

Then, while the family were on vacation, they got a call from a neighbor saying a dog that looked like Arnie was sitting outside their house! It was Arnie, he had returned after nearly two years. The family were delighted, but poor Arnie was in bad shape and had lost a lot of weight.

Arnie is now fit and well and has been introduced to Lucky. The two of them are getting along really well.

Vocabulary

9 Word formation – adjectives to nouns

1 Make nouns from the adjectives in the box using the suffixes to complete the chart.

ill	curious	conscious	free	disappointed
lazy	bored	stupid	strong	exciting
long	wise	moody	generous	

illness	-ness
	-ment
	-dom
	-ity
	-th

2 Complete the sentences using the nouns from exercise 1.

1 Jan regained _consciousness_ after 21 years in a coma, but it'll be a long time before he has the _s_____ to walk again.

2 He died peacefully after a long _i_____ .

3 In a democratic country _f_____ of speech is very important.

4 Look at the fabulous present Ricardo gave me. I can't believe his _g_____ !

5 I've measured the height, width, and _l_____ of the box, and it fits.

6 His advice is always so good. I really appreciate the _w_____ of his words.

7 She can't get over the _d_____ of not getting that job in the bank, but I can't get over the _s_____ of going for the interview in torn jeans.

8 Karen's difficult to live with because of her _m_____ . You never know if she's going to be cheerful or bad-tempered.

9 Don't keep asking questions. You know what they say: "_C_____ killed the cat."

10 You say everything's boring, and you never want to do anything or go anywhere. Your problem is _l_____ not _b_____ . I want some _e_____ in my life!

Prepositions

10 Verb + preposition

1 Complete the sentences with the prepositions in the box.

for (x 4)	on (x 5)	with (x 3)	to (x 2)
of	from	in	about

1. **A** Why are you arguing __with__ the children _____ their allowance again?

   B Well, they spend their money _____ such stupid things.

   A I know, but you have to see it as money that belongs _____ them.

2. Excuse me, this pen doesn't work. Can I exchange it _____ another one?

3. So you're an architect. What are you working _____ at the moment?

4. **A** We fell in love _____ this house as soon as we saw it.

   B I'm not surprised. I've always dreamed _____ having a living room as big as this.

5. I don't believe _____ astrology—not the nonsense they write in the newspapers, anyway.

6. **A** How did Gary react _____ your suggestion?

   B He wasn't excited about the idea.

7. I'm really busy right now – could you deal _____ this inquiry?

8. The train arriving _____ platform 2 is the 5:27 service to Boston. We apologize _____ the late arrival of this train.

9. **A** Excuse me, we didn't ask _____ salad with our pizza.

   B It comes free with every pizza. You don't have to pay _____ it.

10. This book I borrowed _____ Anna is great!

11. I like Martin. I can always rely _____ him to cheer me up when I'm feeling down.

12. I told Barbara that I could easily get the bus home, but she insisted _____ giving me a ride.

Listening

11 Shaksper?

1 Do you think these statements about William Shakespeare are true (✓) or false (✗)?

1. ☐ There's no evidence that he was a writer.
2. ☐ He was a businessman.
3. ☐ He was from an aristocratic background.
4. ☐ He went to college.
5. ☐ His daughters couldn't read or write.

🎧 Listen to the conversation between Jake and his dad and check. Correct the false sentences.

2 Answer the questions.

1. How did Shakespeare spell his name?
2. How much of Shakespeare's background is in the plays?
3. Who was Edward De Vere?
4. Why does his background suggest that he may have written the plays?
5. How many plays were published in De Vere's name?

3 🎧 Listen again and complete the lines from the conversation.

1. … about how he _____ actually written the plays.

2. Well, I think there've always been theories that Shakespeare _____ them.

3. He _____ even worse at spelling than I am.

4. There's so much knowledge in them—well, you _____ that, …

5. But _____ all that information himself?

6. So, who do these people think _____ the plays then?

12

Telling it like it is

Reported speech • Phrasal verbs in context • Ways of talking
• Ways of pronouncing *ou*

Reported speech

1 Reported speech to direct speech

Read the first part of the article. Look at the lines in italics. Guess what Roy Pearson and Soo Chung actually said.

1 "**We can't find the pants.**"

2 "These pants _____."

3 "_____ blue and maroon stripes on them."

4 "_____ because of the style."

5 "The receipt attached to the pants _____."

6 "_____ a victim of fraud!"

7 "_____ emotional damages."

8 "_____ by having a sign in their store that says 'Satisfaction Guaranteed.'"

🎧 Listen and check.

2 Direct speech to reported speech

Read the rest of the article. Report the lines in *italics*.

1 **Customer Lois Ikard said that she thought it was ridiculous.**

2 ABC News's Chris Francescani noted that even ____
_____.

3 Jin Chung mentioned that for two years _____
_____ lawyer fees.

4 The judge said that Pearson _____
_____ to any relief.

5 Jin Chung said that he and his wife _____
_____.

6 Chung added that they _____
_____ finally over.

7 The Chungs' lawyer said that he _____
_____ rest in peace.

The $54 million pants

In 2005, a judge named Roy Pearson brought a pair of pants to a Washington, D.C dry cleaner owned by Soo and Jin Chung. When he went to collect them, the Chungs said that (1) *they couldn't find the pants.*

Two weeks later, they gave Pearson a pair of gray pants, but he claimed (2) *the pants were not his.* (3) *His pants*, he said, *had blue and maroon stripes on them.* But Soo Chung said that (4) *she remembered his gray pants because of the style* and that (5) *the receipt attached to the pants matched Mr. Pearson's receipt.* Even so, the Chungs offered to pay for the pants.

Unsatisfied, Pearson took the Chungs to court. Pearson said that (6) *he had been a victim of fraud* and that (7) *he had suffered emotional damages.* He claimed that (8) *the Chungs were breaking the law* by having a sign in their store that said "Satisfaction Guaranteed." In total, he wanted $54 million!

Anyone could see that Pearson's case was unreasonable. (1) "*I think it's ridiculous,*" said customer Lois Ikard. (2) "*Even fellow trial lawyers are offended,*" noted ABC News's Chris Francescani.

The case was hard on the Chungs. They had to spend a lot of money and close some of their stores. Jin Chung said, (3) "*For two years, we've been paying lawyer fees.*"

In 2007, a judge ruled in favor of the Chungs, saying (4) "*Pearson is not entitled to any relief.*" In response, Jin Chung stated, (5) "*We thank everyone for supporting us.*" He said, (6) "*We hope this nightmare is finally over.*" As for the "Satisfaction Guaranteed" sign, the Chungs are not using it anymore. Their lawyer said, (7) "*I think that sign is going to rest in peace.*"

3 Reporting words and thoughts

1 Report the statements.

1 "I'll miss you very much," he said to her.
   <u>He told her he would miss her very much.</u>

2 "I'm going to Taiwan soon."
   She said _____.

3 "This movie will be interesting."
   I thought _____.

4 "I can't help you because I have too much to do."
   She said _____.

5 "Daniel has bought the tickets."
   I was told _____.

6 "It's a stupid idea, and it won't work."
   She thought _____.

7 "We had terrible weather on our trip."
   He complained _____.

8 "We've never been to Peru," they said to me.
   They told _____.

9 "But we want to go some day," they said.
   They added that _____.

2 Report the questions.

1 "What are you doing?"
   <u>She asked me what I was doing.</u>

2 "Do you want to go for a walk?"
   <u>She asked me if I wanted to go for a walk.</u>

3 "Why are you crying?" he asked her.
   He wondered _____.

4 "Can I borrow your car?"
   He asked me _____.

5 "Where have you come from?"
   The customs officer asked me _____.

6 "How long are you going to be at the gym?"
   She wanted to know _____.

7 "Will you be back early?"
   She asked us _____.

8 "When do you have to go to work?"
   She asked me _____.

9 "How much does it cost to fly to New York?"
   She wanted to know _____.

4 Interview with a bank manager

1 Write the bank manager's questions.

A Come and sit down, Mr. Smith. Now, you want to borrow some money. (1) <u>How much do you want to borrow?</u>

B Five thousand dollars.

A (2) _____?

B Because I want to buy a car.

A I see. Could you give me some personal details?
   (3) _____?

B I'm a graphic designer.

A And (4) _____?

B Sixty thousand dollars a year.

A (5) _____?

B Yes, I am. I've been married for six years.

A (6) _____?

B Yes, we have two children.

A I see you live in an apartment. (7) _____
   _____?

B We've lived there for three years.

A Well, that seems fine. I don't think there'll be any
   problems. (8) _____?

B I'd like it as soon as possible, actually.

A All right. Let's see what we can do.

🎧 Listen and check.

2 Report the bank manager's questions.

1 First, she asked Mr. Smith <u>how much he wanted to borrow</u>.

2 Then she wanted to know _____
   _____.

3 She needed to know _____.

4 He had to tell her _____.

5 Then she asked _____.

6 For some reason, she wanted to know _____
   _____.

7 She asked him _____.

8 Finally, she wondered _____.

Reporting verbs

5 Verb + infinitive

Rewrite the sentences in reported speech. Use the verbs in the box.

persuade	order	ask	~~advise~~	tell
encourage	invite	beg	remind	

1 "If I were you, I'd go to California," he said to me.
   He advised me to go to California.

2 "Could you cook dinner?" he asked Sue.
   _____

3 "Hand in your homework on Monday," the teacher told the class.
   _____

4 "Don't forget to mail the letter," my wife said to me.
   _____

5 "Come over and have dinner with us," Marta said to Paul.
   _____

6 "You must pay a fine of two hundred dollars," the judge said to Stanley Fox.
   _____

7 "Buy the black shoes, not the brown ones," Flora said. "They're much, much nicer."
   "OK," said Emily.
   _____

8 "You should sing professionally," Marco said to Anthony. "You're really good at it."
   _____

9 "Please, please don't tell my father," she said to me.
   _____

6 *ask* and *tell*

> Remember that *ask* can be used to report questions and commands, and *tell* can be used to report statements and commands, but the form is different.
>
> **Questions**
> *She asked me where I lived.*
> *She asked me if I wanted a ride.*
>
> **Statements**
> *He told me he was very unhappy.*
> *He told his wife that he loved her.*
>
> **Commands**
> *He asked me to turn the music down.*
> *She told him to go away.*
>
> Notice the negative command.
> *They asked me not to tell anyone.*
> *She told her son not to worry.*

Rewrite the questions, statements, and commands in reported speech using *ask* or *tell*.

1 "Leave me alone!" she said to him.
   <u>She told him to leave her alone.</u>

2 "Please don't go," he asked her.
   _____

3 "I'm going to bed now," he said to Debra.
   _____

4 "How much do you earn, Dad?" asked Jeremy.
   _____

5 "Turn to page 34," the teacher said to the class.
   _____

6 "Can you call back later, Miss Fulton?" asked the secretary.
   _____

7 "You did very well on the test," said the teacher.
   _____

8 "Don't run across the road!" the police officer told the children.
   _____

9 "Are you going to the concert?" Pam asked Roy.
   _____

10 "It's time to get up!" Harry said to his daughters.
   _____

Vocabulary

7 Ways of speaking

Complete the conversation with the correct form of the verbs in the box.

| say | tell | explain | speak | talk | reply | ask |

I was walking in the park the other day when I met old Mr. Brown, so we stopped and (1) **talked** for a while. He (2) _____ me that his wife, Jenny, had been taken into the hospital. I (3) _____ him how Jenny was, and he (4) _____ that she was getting better. I (5) _____ Mr. Brown to give Jenny my regards. He wondered why I hadn't been to the tennis club recently, so I (6) _____ that I'd been very busy and just hadn't had time.

"There's something you must (7) _____ me," Mr. Brown suddenly said. "How many languages does your son (8) _____ ?"

"Four," I (9) _____. "Why (10) _____ you _____ ?"

"Well, I know your son has some very funny stories to (11) _____ about his trips abroad and his language learning. We're having a meeting of the Travelers' Club next week, and I'd like him to come along and (12) _____ to us."

I (13) _____ that I would (14) _____ to my son about it, and I promised to get back in touch with him.

Then we (15) _____ good-bye and went our separate ways.

8 Other reporting verbs

Rewrite the sentences in reported speech using the verbs in the boxes. Use each verb once.

| complain
admit
deny
suggest
explain | that | | refuse
offer
agree
promise | to do |

1 "I think it would be a very good idea for you to go to bed," the doctor said to Paul.
   The doctor suggested that Paul go to bed.

2 "Yes, OK. I'll lend you $25," Jo said to Matt.
   _____
   _____

3 "Yes, it was me. I broke your camera," said Harry.
   _____
   _____

4 "I didn't pull her hair," said Timmy.
   _____
   _____

5 "I didn't do the homework because I was sick," said the student.
   _____
   _____

6 "If you clean your room, I'll buy you a pizza!" said Jessica's dad.
   _____
   _____

7 "Excuse me! There's a fly in my salad," said Patrick.
   _____
   _____

8 "I'm sorry. I can't marry you because I don't love you," Sarah said to Jento.
   _____
   _____

9 "I'll cook dinner if you like," Amanda said to Kai.
   _____
   _____

Phrasal verbs

9 Phrasal verbs in context (2)

Complete the conversations with the correct form of phrasal verb from the boxes.
The definition in parentheses will help you.

1. A break-in

~~break into~~	show up	get by	get away	go off

A Someone _broke into_ (enter by force) my apartment last night.

B Oh, no! What was stolen? Did they _____ (escape) with much?

A Television, stereo, and my laptop. I don't know how I'm going to _____ (manage to survive) without my laptop.

B Did anyone see or hear anything?

A The alarm _____ (start ringing), but that didn't stop them.

B Did you call the police?

A Yes. They _____ (arrive) about an hour later, but there was nothing really they could do.

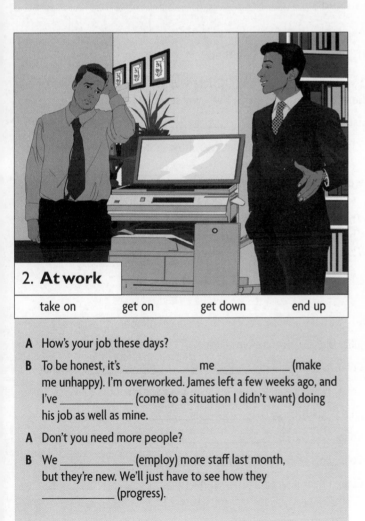

2. At work

take on	get on	get down	end up

A How's your job these days?

B To be honest, it's _____ me _____ (make me unhappy). I'm overworked. James left a few weeks ago, and I've _____ (come to a situation I didn't want) doing his job as well as mine.

A Don't you need more people?

B We _____ (employ) more staff last month, but they're new. We'll just have to see how they _____ (progress).

3. Settling in

pop in	fix up	settle into	look forward to

A Are you _____ (become used to living in) your new apartment?

B Yes. You must _____ (come for a short time) and visit.

A I'd love to. Is there a lot to do to it?

B Oh, yes. We're _____ it _____ (decorate and repair) room by room, so it's a bit of a mess. I'm _____ (want and wait for something good to happen) the time when it's all finished!

A Be patient! You'll get there.

4. Bad luck

run over	beat up	give up	go on

A I'm having a lot of bad luck right now.

B Why? What's _____ (happen)?

A My sister was _____ (hit by a car) outside her house the other day.

B Oh, no! Is she OK?

A Yes, fortunately. But then my brother was _____ (attack and badly hurt) by someone who tried to mug him. He had to go to the hospital.

B How is he now?

A Well, he's _____ (stop doing) his job for the time being. He'll go back to work when he feels better.

Pronunciation

10 Ways of pronouncing *ou*

🎧 The letters *ou* are pronounced in many different ways. For example:

/ɔr/	four	/aʊ/	doubt
/u /	group	/oʊ/	though
/ʌ /	country	/ɪ /	delicious
/ʊ/	would		

▶▶ **Phonetic Symbols p. 93**

1 Choose the word with the different pronunciation.

1 /ʊ/ would should shoulder could
2 /ɔr/ your sour court pour
3 /aʊ/ accountant country count fountain
4 /ɔ/ though ought bought thought
5 /ʌ / enough tough rough cough
6 /ə/ anonymous mouse enormous furious
7 /ʌ / trouble double doubt country
8 /u / through group though soup

🎧 Listen and check.

2 Transcribe the words in phonetic script.

1 It's the /θɔt/_____ that /kaʊnts/_____ .

2 There's an /ɪˈnɔrməs/_____ /maʊs/_____ in the kitchen.

3 I have no /daʊt/_____ that my boss will be /ˈfyʊriəs/_____ .

4 You /ɔt/_____ to do something about that /kɔf/_____ .

5 I have a lot of /ˈtrʌbl/_____ with noisy /ˈneɪbərz/ _____ .

🎧 Listen and check.

Listening

11 *You weren't listening!*

1 Complete these statements as reported speech.

1 "We've run out of brown rice."
   I told you _____

2 "I'll record it for you."
   You said _____

3 "We had a really awful time in Boston last weekend."
   My sister told me today that _____

4 "I went to Washington, DC last weekend, and I think it's one of the most beautiful cities I've ever seen."
   Lisa said that _____

🎧 Listen to an argument between Julia and Colin and check.

2 Answer the questions.
   1 Why was Colin so long at the supermarket?
   2 Why does Julia want brown rice?
   3 Why should they book the train tickets soon?
   4 What's happening in Washington, DC soon?

3 🎧 Listen again and complete the statements.

> **Julia** Did you get some brown rice?
> **Colin** You didn't (1) _____ brown rice.
> **Colin** I never heard you say anything about brown rice.
> **Julia** You obviously (2) _____
> **Colin** You said (3) _____ last week.
> **Colin** Lots of people told (4) _____ .
> **Colin** I think it said in the newspaper (5) _____ .

Vocabulary Crossword 3

Use the clues to complete the crossword. All these words and expressions have appeared in Units 9–12.

ACROSS

3 57% of American adults have a web _____ on Facebook. (4)

5 If a child lives with _____ , he learns to feel worthless. (9)

9 You can't have your chocolate dessert until you _____ up all your spinach. (3)

10 I just watched my team win 6-0. I'm over the _____ ! (4)

12 There was so much traffic, we were _____ a complete standstill for 45 minutes. (2)

13 A doctor will first _____ your illness and then prescribe some medicine. (8)

14 I offered to help Alan but he _____ me to go away! (4)

15 I have a job interview tomorrow. _____ your fingers for me! (5)

19 In most countries you can read and write anything on the Internet— there's no _____ . (10)

20 An _____ is where you sell something to the person who offers the highest price. (7)

21 To _____ honest Jane, I'm not too crazy about your hair that color. (2)

22 I've _____ up with a great new idea for a video game! (4)

24 The title above a story or article in a newspaper is the _____ (8)

27 This part of town used to be very unpopular. Now it's a _____ district filled with busy cafes and restaurants. (8)

28 "Ouch! That hurts!"
"Jane, I thought women have a higher _____ threshold than men." (4)

30 I'm _____ up with waiting at airports. I'm going to travel by train next time! (3)

31 Billy ran away because he didn't feel _____ . (9)

DOWN

1 Another word for shocked is _____ (7)

2 Elvis is known _____ "The King." (2)

4 It's so bright outside, I can't read my book. I need some sun _____ . (7)

6 If you threw $30,000 into the air in my town center, it would certainly start a _____ ! (4)

7 What's the expiration date on your _____ card? (6)

8 Could you spare _____ a minute? I need some help with this crossword. (2)

10 Michelangelo's David is considered to be a _____ . (11)

11 Nowadays many people don't use a teapot to make tea, just a tea _____ in a cup. (3)

16 "It must be true that bats are blind."
"Perhaps, but I'm not _____ sure." (2)

17 I've always hated that office building—I wish they'd _____ it down and build something better. (5)

18 A _____ is the reason why somebody commits a crime. (6)

19 Jimmy Wales and Larry Sanger both _____ to have created Wikipedia. (5)

21 A piece of paper money, like £10 or $50. (8)

23 "How much does a doctor _____ ?"
"About $100,000 a year, I think." (4)

24 Fantastic! Our new website is getting over 1,000 _____ a day! (4)

25 The police can only _____ you if they think you are guilty of a crime. (6)

26 Do you have something I can _____ for a stomach ache? (4)

29 Why did you show _____ so late to the meeting? (2)

Audio Scripts

UNIT 1

Exercise 16, parts 1 and 3

The world of work

I = Interviewer   A = Ayan

I The state of Minnesota is known for its German, Swedish, and Norwegian heritage. But did you know that Minnesota is home to the largest Somali immigrant population in the United States? Here in the studio today is Ayan Ali Shimbir, a young Somali American from Minneapolis, Minnesota, who has started a community center for teenagers. Welcome, Ayan.

A Hello.

I Ayan, were you born in Minnesota?

A No, I wasn't. I was born in Mogadishu, the capital of Somalia.

I When did you first arrive in Minneapolis?

A Well, I came here in 1996 with my parents. I was just a child at the time. We first arrived in Hartford, Connecticut, but my parents had a difficult time finding work there. They heard about the growing Somali community in Minneapolis, and my father had a cousin here, so they came here.

I Why did they come to the United States?

A To chase the American Dream! A better life! But also to get out of Somalia. You may know that in the early 1990s, Somalia was experiencing a terrible civil war. My parents had to leave the country. They wanted a safe place to live and raise their family.

I Minnesota's winters are pretty difficult. It doesn't seem like the kind of place that people from a hot country like Somalia would like to live. Have you and your family learned to love the winter?

A My parents definitely hate the weather, but I try to make the best of it. I've learned how to ski and ice skate! The reason Somalis stay here is because of the community. We help and support each other a lot. For example, if I need money to start a business, I don't go to a bank. I ask someone in the Somali community.

I Somali businesses have been very successful in Minnesota, correct?

A Yes, they have. There is a whole section of Minneapolis called "Little Mogadishu." Hundreds of Somalis own businesses—for example, my father has a shop that sells cell phones and other electronics, and my mother works at her friend's beauty shop.

I Wow. That's interesting!

A The Somali immigrant community has been successful in other ways, too. More and more young Somalis are going to college. The University of Minnesota's Somali Student Association has over 500 members. The community is also producing politicians, writers, artists, photographers … even a movie star!

I Oh, yes, of course! Barkhad Abdi, who won awards for his role in the film Captain Phillips, starring Tom Hanks.

A Abdi's family also left Somalia during the civil war.

I That's a great success story. So what are you doing to help young Somalis succeed in your community?

A Well, although many Somali immigrants have been successful here, a lot of newer immigrants are having a difficult time. Some don't have a very high level of English … many have come here without knowing anyone in the area …

I What about racism—are there any problems with that?

A Yes, there certainly are. A lot of Minnesotans really don't know much about the Somali community, and there's a lot of negative focus in the news and the media. We're trying to change that and increase communication between the Somali community and the local community. We organize cultural events so that Somali teenagers and teenagers from Minnesota and other cultures can share food and music and learn about each other. We also offer a number of different programs and activities to get young Somalis interested and involved in education, art, sports, and nature.

I Do you think you will ever move back to Somalia?

A No, I won't. I've been here most of my life now. I'm Minnesotan! I don't think my parents will either. Their life is here now. Our life is here.

I Thanks so much for joining us today, Ayan.

A Thank you.

UNIT 2

Exercise 13, parts 1 and 3

What's cooking?

L = Linda Davis, presenter
M = Matt Greenberg

L Hello again, and welcome to *What's Cooking?* I'm Linda Davis, and today in the studio we have one of America's best-known and most successful chefs, Matt Greenberg.

M Hi there.

L Matt, you work in one of New York's top hotel kitchens, don't you?

M Yeah, I'm in charge of a great team of chefs there, and I run the kitchen most nights.

L So, what kind of head chef are you then— the typical bad-tempered bully we see on TV, always shouting?

M Mmmm, could be …. Nah, I hardly ever have tantrums, honest! I think running a kitchen does get very stressful if you're passionate about cooking and want to produce the very best, but it actually gives you a real buzz, and I really enjoy the excitement.

L I know what you mean. Now, your background's interesting—you come from England originally, don't you?

M That's right.

L But you're now known for promoting traditional British cooking, which isn't very popular. Why is that?

M Well, I get very frustrated when people say that British cooking isn't very exciting. You know, I tell someone how much I love a good steak pie or a traditional fruit pudding, and they say, "Yeah, fine, but it's all a bit ordinary, isn't it?" Well, I don't agree. I think simple traditional cooking using the best ingredients is never boring and always tasty.

L So, what are you making for us today?

M I'm making a really classic recipe—bread and butter pudding.

L Oh, great—I love bread pudding!

M Yeah, always popular, and it costs next to nothing to make as well. Now, I normally just use raisins in this, but today I'm putting some fresh orange in as well.

L Really? That sounds good. So, you're buttering the bread now—what kind of bread is that?

M It's just an ordinary white loaf, sliced quite thin, with a good sharp bread knife. Right, now I'm heating the milk, cream, and vanilla in a pan, and while that's warming up, I'm whisking the egg yolks and sugar in a bowl.

L How much vanilla extract do you put in?

M I'd say about 5 or 6 drops. And now for the orange—mmm, look at that, a nice organic beauty. These are grown in the Mediterranean, and you can just see all the sunshine that goes into them.

L It does look good, doesn't it? And you're going to peel and chop that?

M No, look, I'm just grating the rind into the raisins.

L OK, and now you're putting the bread into the baking dish.

M That's right, in three layers, with the raisins and orange in between. Now, let's see if that milk's cool enough now—yep, that seems about right—so I'm mixing this into the egg yolks … and now I'm pouring it over the bread. And that's it. Leave it to stand for a while.

L How long?

M About 20–30 minutes, and then put it in the oven for about 30–40 minutes, and that's 350˚F. It needs to be cooked until the top is brown and crispy. Like this one I made earlier.

L Mmm, just the way I like it. Can this be served now?

M You bet!

L Mmmm, that's so good. And people say they don't think much of British cooking …

M Well, they don't know what they're missing, do they?

UNIT 3

Exercise 14, parts 1 and 3

Memories

C = Carol   R = Richard   A = Anne

C Did you see that TV show about memory last night?

R I can't remember.

C Ha ha.

A No, we didn't. We didn't watch TV last night.

C It was really interesting. There was a part about people's earliest memories that I found absolutely fascinating.

R Why's that?

C They were saying that most people have at least one very vivid memory from around the time they were three or three and a half, and quite a few people say they can remember things that happened to them when they were one or two years old.

R I find that hard to believe. Can either of you remember anything that early?

C Yes, I can definitely remember something that happened to me when I was about four. My mom says my dad used to carry me a lot on his shoulders at that age, and I absolutely adored it because he was a really big, tall man.

A Yeah, most children love that, don't they?

C Mmm. So, I think I remember being up there, feeling incredibly high up, much higher than anyone else, and maybe it's one of those memories that you do invent later, but I can imagine it now, feeling literally on top of the world.

But that's not actually the strong memory I'm thinking of. That's of this one day when I was with my mom, dad, and older sister. We were walking through some fields near where we lived, and my dad didn't want to pick me up. I was nagging him to carry me, but he said, "No, you're too big for that now." And I can't remember him ever carrying me after that.

A Oh, that's awful!

C Yeah, it was, because, for me it seemed like the end of childhood, and it was so awful and so sudden.

R And what's your earliest memory then, Anne?

A It's from when I was about two and a half, maybe three years old.

R You're kidding! I just can't believe it's possible to remember anything that early.

A Well, I know this isn't something I've just made up because when I asked my mom, she said it had all really happened like that. It was Christmas Eve, and we had this Christmas tree in the living room, and it was an artificial tree, not a real one, and it was all silvery. And my mom took me in to see it when she'd finished putting the lights and decorations on it, and I remember looking up, standing at the foot of it, and looking up … it seemed … to go on forever … the tallest thing I'd ever seen. And it looked so absolutely fabulous, just magical.

C Oh, I can just imagine it!

A And the thing is, we didn't use this tree for another five years or so, and when we got it out again, and I looked at it, I just couldn't believe that it was the same tree. It was pretty small, only about five feet, but to me as a two-year-old it had seemed at least as high as a house!

C That's nice. That really does show what a completely different world small children live in.

R Yeah, that's a good one. I like that. Maybe I'm just jealous because I don't remember anything about my childhood.

A Well, you probably don't want to remember a time when you definitely didn't know everything!

R Come on, Anne, you know, I've always known everything.

UNIT 4

Exercise 13, parts 1 and 3

A radio call-in

P = Presenter   T = Tony
S = Sarah   A = Andy

P … and it's just coming up to ten minutes past nine and time for our call-in. Today we're asking you which rules you think were made to be broken. And we have Tony, from Brooklyn, on the line. Tony, go ahead.

T I've always hated rules about table manners—drives you crazy. I'll give you an example—you shouldn't put your elbows on the table—why not? Means you can eat more easily, doesn't do any harm, what's the deal?

P You have a point.

T And when you're a kid, you have to eat up everything on your plate. What's that about? If you're full, why should you eat any more? We're actually teaching children to eat too much!

P So, where do you think all this comes from, Tony?

T Dunno. I think people just pick up these rules from their parents—the parents think it's right because they had to do it when they were kids, and then they bring up their own kids the same way. Mindless, stupid rules if you ask me.

P OK, thanks Tony. Sarah, from Manhattan. What rules do you think should be ignored?

S School rules.

P Well, that's a big area. Could you give me an example?

S Yeah, can't leave the school during the day.

P What's wrong with that?

S Well, it's just so random. Why aren't I allowed to leave the school to have lunch? Why do we have to stay there all day, like you're in prison or something?

P Come on, Sarah, they can't let you leave whenever you want.

S Well, maybe younger students shouldn't be allowed, but I don't see why older students can't.

P And why is that so important to you?

S Because you have to have some way of showing responsibility, that's something you should encourage, and … [line goes dead]

P Sarah? Can you hear me? Oh, I'm sorry, it looks like Sarah's been cut off. Well, I think she's going to have to stay in school all day anyway. OK, keep the calls coming in, and do try calling again if you don't get through the first time. Andy, from Queens.

A … when you're driving.

P I'm sorry, we seem to be having a few technical problems today. Would you mind repeating that for me, Andy?

A I said I just read the latest official advice on what you can and can't do when you're driving.

P Oh, yes, it's not just cell phones that aren't allowed now, is it? They're saying you shouldn't eat at the wheel, aren't they?

A Yeah, and apparently you shouldn't read a map or talk to a passenger while you're driving. It even says you shouldn't listen to loud music in the car! Now, I know it's only using a cell phone that's actually illegal, but if you do these other things, it means that the police could charge you for almost anything!

P Well, to be honest Andy, I think the rules on this should be pretty strict. You have to make sure people are concentrating only on the road when they're driving.

A Yeah, but where do you stop? I mean, you can't stop people talking to each other at all in a car, can you? That's ridiculous!

P No, not really—though at least it would stop some of the fights I have with my wife when I'm driving.

A But what about people paying attention to their pets while they're driving? Surely that's more dangerous than talking to someone, and they don't even mention that.

P Yes, well I know these are only guidelines, but I think there's always going to be a lot of debate on this. Anyway, thanks for your call, Andy. Let's take a break there and hear about today's weather …

UNIT 5

Exercise 12, parts 1 and 2

Friends of the earth

D = Debbie   J = Jake   S = Steve
D Hi, Jake!
J Debbie! I thought you were back at school already!
D No, not until next week. And I might go back a bit later anyway.
J Come in.
D Is Steve in as well?
J Yes, he just got up. He's meeting his counselor this afternoon to talk about changing majors.
D Not again! Ah, here he is.
S Hi, Debbie! What are you up to?
D Actually, I was wondering if you two were interested in going to the protest at the airport later this week.
J Mmm, I'd be interested in that.
S I didn't know there was one.
D Well, there isn't yet, but they're setting one up tomorrow.
S So, this is all about the third runway they're planning to build then?
D Ah, at least you've heard about that.
S Well, to be honest, I'm not so sure a protest will make any difference on this one.
D What do you mean?
S Well, I'm pretty sure no one's going to cancel their vacation just because a few people have decided to have their own camping vacation at the airport.
D Steve! I'm never sure whether you just don't get it or you enjoy playing the cynic. It's about generating awareness—it's no good having all this talk about stopping global warming and then saying, "Oh, why don't we expand a few airports?"
J Yeah, come on, Steve. I think there's every chance this protest could make a difference. I've been struck by how people's attitudes have changed after all this strange weather we keep having. I think people are beginning to realize they can't take anything for granted with the climate anymore.
S But you know the figures people keep quoting—air travel only accounts for 5% of carbon dioxide emissions.
J And that it's the fastest growing cause of global warming. It's doubled in the last fifteen years.
S So, what's your prediction then—you think they're going to ban air travel someday soon, do you?
J It's not about banning it. It's just saying that it can't continue growing at this rate.
S Fair enough, I suppose. As long as I'm still allowed one trip a year.
D So, what about coming then?
S Is this protest all legal? I'm not going to get involved in anything illegal or violent.
D I don't know if it's legal or illegal, but I'm sure it will be completely non-violent. They're going to build a proper little eco-village—they're even going to bring wind turbines to power it.

J That's pretty cool. As you always say, every little bit helps.
D Let's do it then. We could drive over there on Tuesday.
S I'm afraid Tuesday's no good for me. What about Wednesday?
J Sounds good to me.
D OK, Wednesday it is. I'll pick you both up at 10:00.

UNIT 6

Exercise 13, parts 1 and 2

My favorite room

L = Laura   D = Dan
L Hey, I hear you have a new house now. What's it like?
D It's great. It feels so good to have more space after living in that tiny apartment.
L Tell me all about it, how big is the new house then?
D Oh, it's not huge or anything, but it's just great to have more rooms, especially when the kids are being noisy. But I must admit, the thing I love most about it is my attic room.
L An attic! That sounds wonderfully old-fashioned! I'd love to have an attic in my house.
D Yes. It's a pretty small space actually, but it's so cozy. It has beautiful, old wooden floorboards, and the walls are a rich dark red color, which makes it feel really warm. I just put some very simple furniture in it— a small coffee table and a little two-seater sofa, not much else really … oh, and a lamp. I love to go up there when I want to read, or even to just sit quietly on my own for a while. It's my own space. Nobody else is allowed in.
L Is it light and airy? What kind of windows does it have?
D Well, there's just one small one in the roof—it has a great view of the park, but only if you stand on the coffee table! But that doesn't matter to me because what I like about being in there is that you feel completely cut off from the world. You haven't lived in your house that long, have you? Do you have a favorite room in it?
L Oh yes, I do—it's my bedroom. I like all the rooms in my house, but my bedroom I just love. It's pretty big, and it has a nice soft wool carpet in it, so it's nice to walk around barefoot. I spent ages trying different color paints on the walls, I must have tried a dozen different colors until I finally found exactly the one I wanted. I think getting just the right color for a room is really important, don't you?
D What color is it?
L Blue. A kind of pale blue but a very warm shade—I know that sounds a bit strange, and blues can be quite cold if you don't choose carefully. I really got into color charts and matching colors when I was doing the room. I even made my own cover for the bed—a patchwork-type thing, using

squares of material in all different matching shades of blue. It brings everything together beautifully.
D Amazing! I didn't know you had such a creative side to you.
L Well, if you can't find anything you like in the stores, you have to get creative, don't you? And the colors do all look gorgeous, even if I say so myself. I also love it because it's such a bright room, even in winter, especially in the morning when the sun shines straight into it. And the window is one of those huge old-fashioned bay windows you can sit in. I had some cushions made for the window seat, which I just love to sit in, and the first thing I do when I get out of bed is sit on there for a while, just staring out into the world. I like to wake up slowly as I watch the first people setting off for work.
D That sounds nice. That's what I meant about being in my attic—it's a space where I can stare into space and daydream for a while. I think we need to do that at some point in the day.
L Yeah. I do sometimes go up there at other times during the day too. There's hardly any furniture in there apart from the wardrobe, just a chair by the bed. The bed's absolutely huge and it's incredibly comfortable to lie on, so I like to take the newspaper and a mug of hot chocolate up there when I get home from work—to escape!
D I'd be worried about falling asleep!
L Well, I do take a 20-minute nap sometimes. It's the same as with you, I need a place where I can go and have some me-time, before I go downstairs to join the chaos that is my wonderful family.

UNIT 7

Exercise 14, parts 1 and 2

Applying for a film degree

C = Counselor   S = Student
C Come in, Jenny. Take a seat.
S Thank you.
C So, you want to find out more about our film courses? Any course in particular?
S Yes. I was thinking of applying for the Degree in Film-Making.
C That's great. Have you read all the admissions requirements? Any questions about those?
S Yes, that's what I wanted to ask about first— what kind of experience do you need to do that program?
C Well, first of all I'll say that all our students are people who've shown they have a real passion for film.
S That's certainly true for me. I've always been crazy about anything to do with film.
C Great. Most of those who start the degree have been making their own films for some time and have worked a lot with other people in the process—teamwork is such an important part of film-making.
S Well, I have made a couple of short films. That was on the program I was doing.

C What program was that? Where did you do it?

S I just finished a part-time Film Studies program at my local college.

C Good for you! Did you find it helpful?

S Yes, it was really informative—is it useful to have a qualification like that?

C Well, it certainly doesn't do any harm, but this is actually a very practical program, not a very academic one! It has to be said, no one's ever been employed in the film industry just because they've completed a course—it's all about practical experience.

S And do your graduates generally manage to get jobs in film?

C Oh yes, they've been employed in all areas of the industry—feature films, TV drama, commercials, pop videos, you name it, they've done it. We have a couple of recent graduates who just released their own low budget feature film, and it's already won an award. In all, about 70% of our recent graduates are working in the business at the moment.

S That's amazing!

C So have you had any experience of directing—camera planning, scheduling, finding and working with actors?

S No, the films I made were real life documentaries, so there wasn't much need for that kind of direction.

C That's a shame. Did you use music on them? The degree has a class on the use of music in film, and you get experience working with a composer.

S Actually, I only had title music on my films—I've never gone into music much.

C OK. Not to worry. Do you have any idea which area of film you'd like to specialize in once you've graduated?

S No, I haven't decided yet. I think I need to know more about all the different areas.

C Fair enough. You know, I'm beginning to think it might be an idea for you to do our Foundation program first, before you think about applying for the degree. That would give you a very good basis for the degree later on.

S What do you do in the Foundation program?

C You learn all the basics—scriptwriting, lighting, camera work, and direction. It'll give you enough experience in each area to decide which one you want to specialize in.

S That sounds like an idea. How long is the program?

C You can do it in a month, during the summer. We're just about to start interviews for that, in May and June—ask for an appointment in reception. I think you'll enjoy it—you should have a lot in common with the other students on that program. We work hard here, but we do make sure we have fun, too!

S Great. I'll go and put my name down for that now. Thanks a lot for your time.

C You're welcome. See you in the summer, I hope. Bye.

S Thanks. I hope so too. Bye.

UNIT 8

Exercise 10, parts 1 and 3

Interview with a stuntwoman

I = Interviewer   C = Carla Simpson

I In this next part of Film Focus, we are going to look at a less well-known aspect of the movie industry—now, we're all familiar with the term "stuntman," but we don't often hear about "stunt*women*." They do exist, of course, and my final guest today is Carla Simpson, who's succeeded in becoming one of Hollywood's top stuntwomen. Hello and welcome, Carla Simpson.

C Thanks.

I So, Carla, tell me, why is it so easy to forget that stuntwomen exist?

C Well, you need to remember that until relatively recently you didn't often see women doing dangerous things in action movies; it was very much a man's world, and if a woman *was* involved, the stunt would still be done by a man.

I What? Dressed up?

C Yes. Well, it's not that difficult to make a man look like a woman, is it? As long as the camera doesn't get too close! But of course these days we expect women to do the stunts, just like the guys, and stuntwomen are actually very much in demand right now. Ever since movies like *Lara Croft Tomb Raider* and the *Matrix* films, there have been lots more high-powered action roles for women, which is great!

I And had you always planned to become a stuntwoman?

C No, I'd never planned to at all—I wanted to be an actor originally. I managed to get into acting school, but I really wasn't very good at it. My teacher knew I was a bit of an adrenaline junkie, and she told me to think about doing stunt work. It just grew from there.

I Were you a bit of a tomboy as a child?

C Oh yes, I was pretty fearless, and I remember climbing trees and jumping off high walls when I was very young. I was always trying to beat the boys, and I've always loved doing extreme sports. That's the great thing—I get paid for doing it now! It's unbelievable!

I So, how do you actually go about becoming a stuntwoman? Are there schools you can go to?

C Not really, it's more a case of finding a trainer to work with. You *do* have to be very highly trained, in an incredible range of skills—driving, and that includes motorcycles, climbing, falling from high buildings, using weapons, then there's fire work, hand fighting, horse work—especially falling off, of course.

I And you have to be able to do *all* those?

C Uh, you don't *have* to, but the more the better. That way you get more work. But most stunt people tend to specialize in one or two areas. For example, I don't mind doing fire work, but I'd rather not do it, whereas I actually enjoy doing high falls.

I But do you ever get scared when you're doing some stunts?

C Well, you know, there's nothing wrong with being afraid of getting hurt badly, and many stunts are life-threatening if they're not fully prepared. That's the key to it, serious preparation. If things aren't properly prepared, I complain, and you need to make sure that everyone is concentrating 100% during a stunt. You minimize the risks.

I Have you been hurt?

C You often get hurt, even on simple stunts, which is why they can't let the actors do them—it's too expensive for them to be off work, even for a day or two. But in the stunt world, we only call it being hurt if you need an ambulance.

I Mmm, it doesn't sound like my idea of fun, I must say.

C Maybe not, but you know, when people ask me about being scared, I always tell them, what really scares me is the idea of wasting your life, not living it to the fullest—that's a truly terrifying thought to me.

I That's a great note to end on. Thanks a lot, Carla.

C Thank you.

UNIT 9

Exercise 12, parts 1 and 2

Scams

E = Elaine   P = Peter

E I bumped into Suzie in town today, and she was telling me …

P Hold on, I'll get that. Hello?
Oh, wonderful, I'm thrilled.
Good-bye.

E Who on earth was that?

P Oh, one of those stupid automated messages. "You have won a prize. Call this number to claim it."

E Oh no. I can't believe anyone would really fall for that. Apparently, if you call back, the prizes are worthless, but they charge you as much as $50 for the call.

P Yeah, I know. There must be plenty of people stupid enough to believe it, otherwise they wouldn't do it, would they?

E I guess not. You know I read somewhere recently that in the U.S. more than five million people lost money to conmen last year.

P That's amazing! There's a guy in my office who got phished last week, and he fell for it.

E Phishing's when they send you fake e-mails, right?

P Yeah, this was one that looked like it was from his bank, saying they needed to update the security details on his account. There was a link that sent him to a website that looked just like his bank's, and of course, he had to enter his old security details before entering new ones.

E Mmm. I must admit, I might have fallen for that one. It's clever, because they're using your insecurity about being conned to con you!

P Yeah. And they can empty your bank account long before you know anything about it.

E Well, someone at my work had his credit card stolen from his jacket, hanging on the back of the office door. He hadn't even noticed, so he was really happy when the bank called him and said that they'd just stopped the criminal trying to use it. Of course, they also wanted to check some security details to make sure it was his card.

P Uh oh! I've guessed what's coming next!

E Yup—he told them his PIN number, and of course, it was actually the thief calling, and he went right away on a very long shopping trip.

P Oh, that's mean. It's obvious a bank would never have asked for his PIN number, but you wouldn't register that at the time, would you? You'd be in a bit of panic after being told that your wallet's been stolen.

E Absolutely. It's useful to hear about these scams, though, isn't it? I mean, if they tried that one on *me* now, at least I'd know about it.

P Yeah. Well, the best one I've ever seen was on that TV show where they film actors doing scams on the public. This actor, a big guy, walks into a museum wearing a black suit and a white shirt and stops in a corridor in the middle of the museum. Out of his pocket he pulls a security guard's cap and an official-looking badge, which he hangs around his neck. And he starts stopping people and says he has to check them, searching their pockets for anything dangerous.

E And somehow I suspect there was less in their pockets at the end of the search?

P That's right. He got three wallets full of cash and credit cards in about five minutes. And it was a long time before any of them noticed, because they were walking around the rest of the museum.

E You see, I would have believed him, definitely. It's the authority thing with people in a uniform, you just obey them automatically.

P Yeah, and even if somewhere inside you did feel a little suspicious, you wouldn't want to make a scene in public, would you?

E Certainly not! But honestly, if we're not careful, we'll end up being suspicious of everyone. Still, I suppose it's good to keep your guard up.

UNIT 10

Lost and found

M = Mark   A = Amy

M Hi, Amy! How's it going?

A Hi, Mark. Oh, OK. I'm just a little annoyed with myself because I left my umbrella on the bus. It was a really good one too.

M Someone might hand it in, you never know.

A Oh, I doubt it. And anyway, it's such an effort to go to the Lost and Found office—and I don't even know where it is—and there's probably loads of paperwork involved in getting it back.

M Well, you're in luck. I have a friend who works in the bus station, and I think he has to deal with lost property sometimes. I can give him a call, and if it's been handed in, he could have it ready for you to pick up.

A Aw, that would be great, thanks.

M So, which umbrella should I tell him to look out for—the pink girlie one I assume?

A Yes, of course—it's a Barbie umbrella. Actually, it's a very classy-looking black and white umbrella with a silver point. It's pretty big—it looks like a golfing umbrella. And … it has a white handle with a black stripe down the side of it.

M Excuse me! I'll wait a couple of hours and then I'll call him.

A I bet they get loads of umbrellas left on buses, don't they?

M Yeah. I think it might be the most common thing, I can't remember. I read something on the Internet a couple of weeks ago about the things that people most often leave on public transportation. Let me see if I can find it again … Yes, here it is. Ah, umbrellas are number three on the list. What do you think is the most common?

A Bags?

M Oooh, close. That's number two—especially shopping bags. Yeah, I've done that—put it on the floor under your feet, and you've forgotten all about it by the time you get off.

A Is it sunglasses?

M Well, it doesn't say *sun*glasses, but glasses in general are fourth on the list.

A I can't think what it is then.

M Coats and jackets.

A Oh, that does surprise me. They seem too big to forget about, and you wouldn't put them on the floor. What about cell phones? Are they on the list?

M Yup, they're number five. [*laughs*] It says that they leave them switched on so that people can call them, but everyone who calls in thinks that the person who's answering is a thief, so they get a lot of abuse at first! Now, what about laptops?

A Surely people don't leave those on buses and trains very often, do they?

M Well, they're not on this list. But the article says there is a place where laptops are often lost. See if you can guess where it is.

A Taxis?

M No—it's airports.

A What? In the departure gate?

M No. It sounds unbelievable, but it's people forgetting to pick their laptops up again after they've put them through the X-ray machine.

A No! And I thought I was stupid. I'd never forgive myself if I did that.

M Oh, come on, it is a pretty stressful time, sorting out your coat, cell phone, belt, shoes, money—and all those security guards staring at you. People can't get out of there quick enough.

A But they must realize they've left them behind before long. Why don't they just go back and ask?

M Maybe they don't have time to go all the way back to the X-ray machines by the time they've realized. And it says that like you, most people don't even contact Lost and Found about it—they just assume someone will have stolen it.

A It's terrible how little we trust each other these days, isn't it? Anyway, we'll see. If someone hands my umbrella in, I'll promise to have more faith in human nature.

UNIT 11

Dear Ruth,

I am fourteen years old, and I have a big problem with my younger brother, Cal, who's 8. We fight all the time. It's terrible, I know, but I think I hate him. He follows me everywhere, and he wants to use all my things, especially my computer. He ruins everything I'm doing. If I'm with my friends, he always wants to be with us, and when I tell him to go away he goes crying to our mother. My parents always take his side. He's so spoiled he gets everything he wants. My mom says she can't understand why I don't want him with me and my friends, but we can't talk freely with him hanging around all the time. My dad says I should play with him more and let him use my computer, but he just plays his silly games on it and screams if I want to use it for my school work. He doesn't have many friends. Nobody at his school likes him, and I know why—he cries if he doesn't win every game, and he fights with the other children. My parents think he can do no wrong. What can I do?
Yours,
Luke Basset

Dear Ruth,

My husband and I and our two sons are a happy and loving family. Ten months ago, after years of saving our money, we moved to the house of our dreams. However, our lives are now being made miserable by the behavior of our neighbors, Mr. and Mrs. Fletcher. They play loud music until late at night. It's so loud that our children can't sleep. When we asked them to turn it down they refused. They don't have any children, and they say that ours make too much noise when they're playing in the backyard. Also, they have refused to cut the hedge on their side of the fence. It is now huge and stops all the sunlight getting into our backyard. One of the reasons we bought the house was because of the beautiful backyard, and now we can't use it. We've tried to talk to them about this too, but they say that they can do what they want in their backyard. We don't want to move, but we're going crazy. What can we do?
Yours,
Jane Iverson

Shaksper?

J = Jake   D = Dad

J Dad, can you help me with my English homework?

D Sure, what's it on?

J We're doing *Romeo and Juliet*.

D Ah, that's funny. I was listening to a radio program on Shakespeare in the car today. And how he might not have actually written the plays.

J You're kidding!

D No. Do they ever talk about that at school?

J No.

D Well, I think there've always been theories that Shakespeare couldn't have written them—and to be honest—I did find this program pretty convincing, even though I haven't read any of his plays since I was in school.

J But look, it says here in black and white, *Romeo and Juliet* by William Shakespeare. Must be true.

D Not really. Don't believe everything you read. They said on this program that no one can come up with any hard evidence that Shakespeare was a writer—there are documents referring to him but only as an actor and a businessman. And apparently he didn't write his name like that—he spelled it in different ways, but in all his signatures it's "Shaksper"—S-H-A-K-S-P-E-R.

J That's funny actually, because I can never remember if there's an "e" at the end of his name or not. He could just have been even worse at spelling than I am.

D No, that's not possible, Jake. But some people argue that Shakespeare couldn't have had the education you'd need to write all those plays. There's so much world knowledge in them—well, you must know that from having to work out all the references, you know, to history, law, music, Italian culture, all the foreign languages in them. But Shakespeare was from a pretty ordinary background, you know, so at best he must have gone to the local grammar school and left at sixteen. He never went to college.

J Really? But weren't universities just for aristocrats in those days anyway? And didn't they study weird subjects too?— Latin and astronomy—ugh!

D Yeah, well, of course, you're right—very few people did go in those days and yes, ordinary people weren't allowed to go.

J But couldn't he have found out all that information for himself some other way?

D What, on the Internet?

J Yeah, ha ha, alright, it wouldn't have been so easy.

D And the other thing is, there's nothing in the plays about Shakespeare's own background, you know, Stratford, stuff from his own life.

J Well, writers do make things up when they're writing, Dad.

D Yeah, but there's always *something* that comes from their own life. With Shakespeare, nothing we can see. And—this I did find amazing—apparently Shakespeare's own daughters couldn't read or write! Not what you'd expect from a literary genius, is it?

J So who do these people think must have written these plays then?

D Um, what was his name? Edward somebody … De Vere, I think, the Earl of Oxford.

J Is there any proof?

D Not really, but they said there's a lot in the plays that's similar to events in *his* life, and being an aristocrat, he would have had the right background, university, lots of foreign travel.

J And was he definitely a writer then?

D Well, apparently there are lots of documents referring to him as a writer of great poems and plays, but there isn't a single play published in his name. That's the big flaw in the argument.

J Right. Well, at least I can forget this homework now.

D What do you mean?

J Well, they can't expect me to write an essay on Shakespeare's style if they can't even prove he wrote this play, can they?

D Mmm. I don't think they'll buy that argument at school—remember it's only a theory, and there's no proof that Shakespeare *didn't* write the plays. Sorry, Jake, come on, let's have a look at what you have to write.

UNIT 12

You weren't listening!

J= Julia   C = Colin

J Oh, you're back. You've been gone forever. What were you up to?

C The supermarket was absolutely packed. I'd forgotten Friday night is always so crowded.

J Well, rather you than me. Did you get the brown rice?

C No, I got white rice. You didn't say you wanted brown.

J Yes, I did. I distinctly remember saying it to you as you went out. Anyway, that's what this recipe says we have to use.

C I never heard you say anything about brown rice.

J But I did. I told you that we'd run out of brown rice and I needed it for this … Oh, never mind! You obviously weren't listening to me—again.

C Yes, I was, honestly. I just don't remember you saying anything about brown rice.

J You just don't listen to me. Don't deny it.

C Well, that's not true—or at least only when you're nagging.

J I presume that means whenever I complain about anything. Then I'm nagging and being unreasonable.

C Well, sometimes you *can* be a little unreasonable when we argue.

J Oh, so it's unreasonable to criticize you, is it?

I am so sure I asked you to get brown rice, but you're never going to admit you weren't listening—as usual! Oh look—we just seem to be going around in circles again! Let's forget it.

C Alright, I'm sorry, we all make mistakes, and we're both tired and hungry after a long day at work. Let's just eat and then watch TV. Did you record my show?

J Sorry, what show? You didn't say you wanted me to record anything.

C But you said you'd record it for me.

J Well, come on, you didn't remind me to. Honestly, I can't remember everything, you know.

C True!

J Look, I'm sorry—let's just stop! I hate it when we argue like this.

C Me too. Anyway, I can live without my show I suppose. Maybe I'll go online and book that weekend in Boston we were talking about.

J Ah, I meant to say earlier—I've changed my mind about that.

C What do you mean?

J Well, you see, I was talking to Jane today and she told me that she and Fred had had a really awful time in Boston last weekend. She said the weather was absolutely terrible—freezing cold and wet.

C Does it really matter what your sister and her boring husband think? Lots of people have told me that Boston's a wonderful place. It has so much, the buildings, the atmosphere …

J I know, I know. It's just that I'd rather wait until it's a bit warmer. We could go in the summer—maybe for the Fourth of July. Actually, Lisa at work said that she'd been to Washington, DC last weekend, and she thought it was one of the most beautiful cities she'd ever seen. And there's lots to do and see.

C OK, I give in! But you better make up your mind soon, you know if we don't book soon, the train tickets will be very expensive. We have to book three weeks before we want to go to get the best price.

J OK, where do *you* want to go?

C I suppose I don't really mind. Let's go to Washington, DC then. It is supposed to be really nice. I think it said in the newspaper that there was a festival there next month. That might be worth going to. I'll check that out, and maybe we can decide when we'd like to go.

J Great. Thanks, darling. Oh, Colin, would you like a brown rice salad made with white rice?

C Sounds wonderful. All that arguing has made me hungry!

Verb Patterns

Verbs + -ing	
adore can't stand don't mind enjoy finish imagine loathe	doing swimming cooking

Note

We often use the verb *go + -ing* for sports and activities.
> I **go swimming** every day.
> I **go shopping** on weekends.

Verbs + preposition + -ing	
give up look forward to succeed in think of	doing

Verbs + to + infinitive	
afford agree choose dare decide expect forget help hope learn manage mean need offer plan promise refuse seem want would hate would like would love would prefer	to do to come to cook

Notes

1 *Help* and *dare* can be used without *to*.
> We **helped clean up** the kitchen.
> They didn't **dare disagree** with him.

2 *Have to* for obligation.
> I **have to wear** a uniform.

3 *Used to* for past habits.
> I **used to eat greasy food**, but I stopped last year.

Verbs + sb + to + infinitive		
advise allow ask beg encourage expect force help invite need order persuade remind tell want warn would like	me him them someone	to do to go to come

Note

Help can be used without *to*.
> I **helped** him **do** the dishes.

Verbs + sb + infinitive (no *to*)		
help let make	her us	do

Notes

1 *To* is used with *make* in the passive.
> We were **made to work** hard.

2 *Let* cannot be used in the passive. *Allowed to* is used instead.
> She was **allowed to leave**.

Verbs + *-ing* or *to* + infinitive (with little or no change in meaning)	
begin continue hate like love prefer start	doing to do

Verbs + *-ing* or *to* + infinitive (with a change in meaning)	
remember stop try	doing to do

Notes

1 *I **remember mailing** the letter.*
      (= I have a memory now of a past action: mailing the letter.)

   *I **remembered to mail** the letter.*
      (= I reminded myself to mail the letter. I didn't forget.)

2 *I **stopped drinking** coffee.*
      (= I gave up the habit.)

   *I **stopped to drink** a coffee.*
      (= I stopped doing something else in order to have a cup of coffee.)

3 *I **tried to** sleep.*
      (= I wanted to sleep, but it was difficult.)

   *I **tried counting** sheep and **drinking** a glass of warm milk.*
      (= These were possible ways of getting to sleep.)

Irregular Verbs

Base form	Past form	Past participle	Base form	Past form	Past participle
be	was/were	been	eave	left	left
beat	beat	beaten	lend	lent	lent
become	became	become	let	let	let
begin	began	begun	lie	lay	lain
bend	bent	bent	light	lighted/lit	lighted/lit
bite	bit	bitten	lose	lost	lost
blow	blew	blown	make	made	made
break	broke	broken	mean	meant	meant
bring	brought	brought	meet	met	met
build	built	built	must	had to	had to
buy	bought	bought	pay	paid	paid
can	could	been able	put	put	put
catch	caught	caught	read /rid/	read /red/	read /red/
choose	chose	chosen	ride	rode	ridden
come	came	come	ring	rang	rung
cost	cost	cost	rise	rose	risen
cut	cut	cut	run	ran	run
dig	dug	dug	say	said	said
do	did	done	see	saw	seen
draw	drew	drawn	sell	sold	sold
dream	dreamed	dreamed	send	sent	sent
drink	drank	drunk	set	set	set
drive	drove	driven	shake	shook	shaken
eat	ate	eaten	shine	shone	shone
fall	fell	fallen	shoot	shot	shot
feed	fed	fed	show	showed	shown
feel	felt	felt	shut	shut	shut
fight	fought	fought	sing	sang	sung
find	found	found	sink	sank	sunk
fit	fit	fit	sit	sat	sat
fly	flew	flown	sleep	slept	slept
forget	forgot	forgotten	slide	slid	slid
forgive	forgave	forgiven	speak	spoke	spoken
freeze	froze	frozen	spend	spent	spent
get	got	got	spoil	spoiled	spoiled
give	gave	given	spread	spread	spread
go	went	been/gone	stand	stood	stood
grow	grew	grown	steal	stole	stolen
hang	hanged/hung	hanged/hung	stick	stuck	stuck
have	had	had	swim	swam	swum
hear	heard	heard	take	took	taken
hide	hid	hidden	teach	taught	taught
hit	hit	hit	tear	tore	torn
hold	held	held	tell	told	told
hurt	hurt	hurt	think	thought	thought
keep	kept	kept	throw	threw	thrown
kneel	knelt	knelt	understand	understood	understood
know	knew	known	wake	woke	woken
lay	laid	laid	wear	wore	worn
lead	led	led	win	won	won
learn	learned	learned	write	wrote	written

Phonetic Symbols

Consonants

1	/p/	as in	**pen** /pɛn/	9	/s/	as in	**son** /sʌn/	17	/w/	as in	**want** /wɒnt/
2	/b/	as in	**big** /bɪg/	10	/z/	as in	**zoo** /zu/	18	/θ/	as in	**thanks** /θæŋks/
3	/t/	as in	**tea** /ti/	11	/l/	as in	**live** /lɪv/	19	/ð/	as in	**the** /ðə/
4	/d/	as in	**do** /du/	12	/m/	as in	**my** /maɪ/	20	/ʃ/	as in	**she** /ʃi/
5	/k/	as in	**cat** /kæt/	13	/n/	as in	**nine** /naɪn/	21	/ʒ/	as in	**television** /ˈtɛlɪvɪʒn/
6	/g/	as in	**go** /goʊ/	14	/h/	as in	**happy** /ˈhæpi/	22	/tʃ/	as in	**child** /tʃaɪld/
7	/f/	as in	**five** /faɪv/	15	/r/	as in	**red** /rɛd/	23	/dʒ/	as in	**Japan** /dʒəˈpæn/
8	/v/	as in	**very** /ˈvɛri/	16	/y/	as in	**yes** /yɛs/	24	/ŋ/	as in	**English** /ˈɪŋglɪʃ/

Vowels

25	/i/	as in	**see** /si/	33	/u/	as in	**you** /yu/	41	/ər/	as in	**bird** /bərd/
26	/ɪ/	as in	**his** /hɪz/	34	/ʌ/	as in	**sun** /sʌn/	42	/ir/	as in	**near** /nir/
27	/ɛ/	as in	**ten** /tɛn/	35	/ə/	as in	**about** /əˈbaʊt/	43	/ɛr/	as in	**hair** /hɛr/
28	/æ/	as in	**stamp** /stæmp/	36	/eɪ/	as in	**name** /neɪm/	44	/ɑr/	as in	**car** /kɑr/
29	/ɑ/	as in	**father** /ˈfɑðər/	37	/aɪ/	as in	**my** /maɪ/	45	/ɔr/	as in	**more** /mɔr/
30	/ɔ/	as in	**saw** /sɔ/	38	/ɔɪ/	as in	**boy** /bɔɪ/	46	/ʊr/	as in	**tour** /tʊr/
31	/ɒ/	as in	**hot** /hɒt/	39	/aʊ/	as in	**how** /haʊ/				
32	/ʊ/	as in	**book** /bʊk/	40	/oʊ/	as in	**go** /goʊ/				

OXFORD
UNIVERSITY PRESS

198 Madison Avenue
New York, NY 10016 USA

Great Clarendon Street, Oxford, OX2 6DP, United Kingdom

Oxford University Press is a department of the University of Oxford.
It furthers the University's objective of excellence in research, scholarship,
and education by publishing worldwide. Oxford is a registered trade
mark of Oxford University Press in the UK and in certain other countries

© Oxford University Press 2016

The moral rights of the author have been asserted

First published in 2016

2020 2019 2018 2017 2016

10 9 8 7 6 5 4 3 2 1

No unauthorized photocopying

ISBN: 978 0 19 472615 3
WORKBOOK (PACK COMPONENT)
ISBN: 978 0 19 472614 6
WORKBOOK (PACK)
ISBN: 978 0 19 472623 8
ICHECKER (PACK COMPONENT)
ISBN: 978 0 19 472627 6
WORKBOOK ACCESS CARD (PACK COMPONENT)

Printed in China

This book is printed on paper from certified and well-managed sources

ACKNOWLEDGEMENTS

*The publisher is grateful to those who have given permission to reproduce the following
extracts and adaptations of copyright material:* p.11 "How trolley girl read the
market to become queen of fast", The Times, 25/08/2007. © NI Syndication
2007

Illustrations by: Jonathan Burton pp.40, 61; Gill Button pp.14, 48, 54, 68; Leo
Hartas p.53; Belle Mellor pp.20, 26, 46, 76; Dettmer Otto pp.4; Roger Penwill
pp.31, 32, 72, 73; Gavin Reece pp. 12, 25, 81.

*The publishers would like to thank the following for permission to reproduce
photographs:* Cover- Paul Harizan/Getty Images(2), Ralf Hiemisch/fstop/
Corbis; Global-OUP/Digital Vision; p.2 Jade/Blend Images/Corbis, Kevin
Dodge/Getty Images, Juice Images/Alamy Stock Photo, Songquan Deng/
Shutterstock; p.5 Erica Shires/Corbis; p.7 Jahi Chikwendiu/The Washington
Post via Getty Images; p.8 Jim Purdum/Getty Images; pp.8–9 Zoonar GmbH/
Alamy Stock Photo; p.11 jeremy sutton-hibbert/Alamy Stock Photo(2);
p.15 Joff Lee Studios/AGE fotostock; p.16 Graeme Massie/Splash News/
Corbis; p.17 Hero Images/Corbis, Kristy Viera/Shutterstock, alice-photo/
shutterstock; p.19 mimagephotography/shutterstock, Minerva Studio/
shutterstock; p.21 Fabrizio Bensch/Reuters/Corbis; p.22 Taisa/shutterstock;
p.23 OUP/Shutterstock/Critterbiz; p.24 OUP/Image Source, Image Source/
Alamy Stock Photo, Fotoluminate LLC/shutterstock; p.27 145/Scott Quinn
Photography/Ocean/Corbis; p.30 AP Photo/Rich Pedroncelli, Marty Bicek/
ZUMA Press/Corbis, Citizen of the Planet/Alamy Stock Photo; pp.33, 34
Maskot/Getty Images; p.35 OUP/Photodisc; p.36 Tim Pannell/Corbis; p.38
OUP/KidStock; p.39 Courtesy of Suzannah Kolbeck; p.43 Danny E. Martindale/
Getty Images, Laura Cavanaugh/Getty Images, Imago/ZUMA Press/Newscom,
Alfred Eisenstaedt/Pix Inc./The LIFE Picture Collection/Getty Images, Michael
Putland/Getty Images, Roger Ressmeyer/Corbis, Dimitrios Kambouris/
Getty Images for Tiffany & Co., Popperfoto/Getty Images; p.44 D Dipasupil/
FilmMagic/Getty Images, Joe Stevens/Retna Ltd./Corbis; p.45 Cultura/
yellowdog/Getty Images; p.47 Andrew Wilson/Loop Images/superstock;
p.50 MIVA Stock/superstock; pp.50-51 Juniors Bildarchiv/AGE fotostock;
p.51 Biosphoto/superstock; p.55 Image Point Fr/shutterstock, visual7/Getty
Images; p.57 Tom Grill/Blend Images/Corbis; p.59 Sean Locke Photography/
shutterstock, Commercial Eye/Getty Images; p.60 Andresr/shutterstock,
40260/Getty Images; p.64 Courtesy of One Laptop Per Child (www.laptop.
org); p.65 Keystone-France/Gamma-Keystone via Getty Images; p.69 Gyvafoto/
shutterstock, Evgeny Karandaev/shutterstock, fashionall/shutterstock,
OUP/Shutterstock/Umberto Shtanzman, OUP/Leonid Nyshko; p.70 Radius
Images/Corbis; p.74 Blaine Harrington III/Corbis; p.75 Marvin Dembinsky
Photo Associates/Alamy Stock Photo; p.77 Jason Reed/Reuters/Corbis; p.78
Wavebreak Media ltd/Alamy Stock Photo; p.80 imageBROKER/Alamy Stock
Photo; p.82 wavebreakmedia/shutterstock.